GHOST STORIES
OF
CENTRAL
NEW MEXICO

CODY POLSTON

Haunted
America

Published by Haunted America
A Division of The History Press
Charleston, SC
www.historypress.com

First published 2024

Manufactured in the United States

ISBN 9781467157582

Library of Congress Control Number: 2024935299

CONTENTS

PREFACE

Since childhood, I have loved tales about the supernatural and the paranormal, which eventually led to a fascination with horror films. Why do I love ghost stories? Because, like horror movies, they provide a temporary sort of terror, yet you know you are safe. People go to horror films because they want to be frightened; otherwise, they wouldn't do it twice. You choose your entertainment because you want it to affect you. I can watch a horror film like *Nightmare on Elm Street* and enjoy it, even though I know the film's villain, Freddy Krueger, isn't real. The same is true with ghost stories. I really appreciate them, especially if some historical element is attached to the story.

However, like in horror movies, if the conversation changes to a discussion about whether the stories are true, that is another matter. In that regard, ghost stories must be taken with a grain of salt. One characteristic that distinguishes ghost stories from other folklore is that they emphasize the mystery and the inconclusive, which invites various kinds of interpretation. From my perspective, the answer to the question "Do you believe?" belongs to the people who are telling or listening to a story about a paranormal experience. They decide whether they want to believe or even if they're going to engage with it concerning any type of belief at all.

I take paranormal narratives seriously. I pay attention to how they are created, why some last and others are forgotten and how they change over time with different storytellers.

It is essential to understand the difference between ghost stories and personal paranormal encounters. Ghost stories are just that—stories. They revolve around a central character that usually undergoes some traumatic event, explaining why they are haunting a particular location. Ghost stories are told with a dramatic fervor with spooky anecdotes and ambiance. They primarily serve as entertainment and depend on the storyteller's ability to be effective. However, personal paranormal encounters are quite different. Typically, they are told reluctantly and with an apology. The teller is often aware that such admissions are considered the delusions of a troubled mind and is mindful of being judged. Of course, there is no actual witness stand. Yet people who have these encounters are conscious of the possibility of being judged irrationally and assume a stance that anticipates the skepticism of their observations and conclusions. In these instances, I do not doubt that these people have had an experience. Obviously, they did, but it is their interpretation of the circumstances and the environment that I tend to ponder and open up for discussion. Many of the supernatural tales in this book combine both types. They are ghost stories that are mixed with personal paranormal encounters. As such, I have included additional insights for more inquisitive readers. I hope you enjoy reading about these fascinating places as much as I did researching and writing about them.

1

OLD GHOST STORIES AND URBAN LEGENDS

I'm a fan of ancient accounts, stories that were shared at one time and then vanished. They offer a glimpse into the strange tales that cast fear into the people of those bygone days. One is a story titled "A Haunted House," and was published in the *Las Vegas Optic* on August 22, 1899. In it, a man identified only as Mr. Wilson reported to the Springer newspaper that the cabin of Harry Lyons, located near Elizabethtown, was haunted by a ghost.

Wilson declared that he had been securing the windows and doors of Lyons's cabin for a month, only to find them wide open each time he returned. The newspaper added:

> *Some stuff in the house was moved around on different occasions, noises of a strange nature were heard, the laugh of Mr. Lyons, some two years dead, could be plainly heard, his whistle, talk, etc.*

Wilson added that everyone in the area was afraid to go near the cabin. Strange things were happening even in his own yard, Mr. Wilson continued. He said a cowbell was lying in his yard, and one day, his children heard it ring. Thinking their father was fastening the bell to one of the horses, the children walked out into the yard, only to find that the cowbell was still on the ground, and nobody was around.

The newspaper article reported that Wilson would attest to all the strange occurrences that had been occurring in the area.

He says that heretofore he has not been a believer in spirits of any kind, either fermented or those of the departed, but he does believe there is something of that kind around the Lyon cabin now.

The second ghost story, titled "The Ghost of the Canyon," was published in the *Albuquerque Democrat* on November 12, 1889. According to historians, this tale was a favorite among prospectors. It is said that the Pueblo Natives of the Middle Rio Grande valley passed the story down through generations.

During the Pueblo Revolt of 1680, a Spanish colonist named Ramon Vigil allegedly trekked to the north edge of the Sandia Mountains and hid treasure worth $250,000. The Natives seized Vigil and tortured him in the hopes that he would give away the hiding place of his treasure. Despite their efforts, he died with his secret kept safe.

Sometime later, a lone Pueblo Native, caught in a heavy storm in the Sandias, sought refuge behind some rocks in a canyon and attempted to start a fire. Suddenly, the storm ceased, and a bright moon shone forth from behind the clouds, making the Native very happy. "But his happiness was of short duration," the article continued.

The air became oppressive, and he could scarcely breathe. He attempted to leave the spot but could not move. A spell seemed to be upon him, and while in this condition, Ramon Vigil, the man whom he had seen so cruelly put to death a short time before, appeared before him. He beckoned the savage to follow, and together they proceeded to the top of the mountain.

When Vigil and the Pueblo Native reached the summit, Vigil gestured to the man to enter a cave beneath an overhanging tree branch. It was almost invisible among the shrubs of the mountaintop. The Native, accompanied by the spirit, descended into a tunnel that seemed to go on forever. It eventually led to an enormous cave that was hidden beneath the mesa. There, the spirit left the Pueblo Native, who fell to the floor unconscious and overcome with fright.

When he awoke, the Pueblo Native found himself in a pitch-black environment. He scraped together some kindling and lit a flame, which provided at least some illumination. The sight that greeted him was one of the grandest that ever befell the lot of man.

Vigil's treasure was before him, but it was like a water drop compared to a mighty river. The cave walls were a mass of dazzling gold that were blinding

Does the ghost of Ramon Vigil guard a treasure hidden in the Sandia Mountains? *Wikimedia Commons.*

in their brightness. On the floor were piled nuggets and boulders of gold so large and heavy that a dozen men could not lift one of them.

The Pueblo Native explored the cave's depths for hours before discovering a passageway upward. He ascended a flight of stairs made entirely of gold before he emerged outside. He then marked his location so he could remember it later. Then he journeyed back to his home in the Rio Grande Valley.

Later, bands of people from the man's Pueblo village scoured the Sandias Mountains, desperately trying to find Vigil's treasure—but to no avail. The article concluded:

> *The Indians now tell the story, but among all the Pueblos, there is not one who will go near the spot, for they say that it is guarded by the ghost of Ramon Vigil, who never appears except during an awful storm in the mountains.*

The ghost of a Spaniard at Quarai is the subject of another old ghost story that has appeared in the local newspapers. It tells of an Illinois man and his family who were on a journey in a prairie schooner in New Mexico when they camped at the Quarai Mission ruins near the village of Punta de Agua, not too far from Mountainair. This church was erected sometime in 1629 but was deserted by the 1670s.

The Illinois family packed up their camp at Quarai and headed farther east to the small settlement of Willard. On November 27, 1913, the head of the family released a statement regarding their journey.

My name is Wilbur S. Saener, and my home is near Minonk, Ill. My wife's health was not of the best, so I resolved to bring her and my little daughter out here to your healthful state of New Mexico, roughing it as you see, and I thank the good Lord that we did come for my wife's health has entirely restored. I have traveled by covered wagon to many parts of your state, including Albuquerque, El Paso, Belen, and many other points.

We were told of the church ruins at Punta de Agua, so we resolved to see the ruins of the structure, built so many hundreds of years ago.

We camped two nights at the old mission, and many were the thoughts of a religious turn that passed through our minds as we lay there at night and gazed into the shadows of the ruins of this house of worship.

Nothing occurred the first night out of the ordinary, but what I saw on the second night will always remain fresh in my memory. My family or myself will never be able to blot it from memory.

I was restless for some reason and got up, and through one of the openings in the end of the ruined edifice I saw a brilliant blue-white light, and in the center of the light stood the figure of a man, apparently a Spaniard, but dressed in the uniform of a French soldier.

Thinking my eyes deceived me, I called my family, and they, too, saw the ghostly light and soldier. Three times he pointed a finger and said, "Siste, visitor," the Latin for "Stop, visitor." And of a sudden, the light and the man disappeared.

Saener's statement, given here in its entirety, was published in the *Albuquerque Evening Herald* on November 28, 1913. The headline over the statement read, "Ghost of Old Spaniard Haunts Punta de Agua."

One dark night years ago, I sat just outside the front entrance of the Quarai Mission church ruins until about 2:00 a.m., waiting for this ghost to appear, but I saw no sign of him.

Rumor has it that the Quarai ghost appears only during a full moon. However, no one I know has seen this spectral figure, so I wonder why people believe the lunar cycle is associated with it. Additionally, I'm

Quarai Mission ruins near the village of Punta de Agua. *Wikimedia Commons.*

bewildered about why a Spanish specter would be wearing French garb and speaking in Latin.

Apart from those tales of terror and excitement, there are other, less well-known legends that used to give shivers to those who heard them. They were published in the *Albuquerque Journal* on October 30, 1979, by Fritiz Thompson.

THE PHANTOM OF THE ARROYO

If you're a weekend treasure hunter, and if you tramp into the Sangre de Cristos near Pecos, be prepared to encounter a mounted gentleman wearing a sombrero and buckskin breeches and to be ordered from the vicinity by a strangely disembodied voice in the hills.

At the head of one of the innumerable arroyos that crease the mountains lies a cave or, as some describe it, a mine shaft. Inside are several rusting chests of Spanish treasure, containing everything from coins to gold and a silver candelabra.

One man, who claims to have accidentally stumbled on the cache, says he was frightened away by the sudden appearance of a Spanish grandee astride a horse at the rim of the arroyo. The man wore a black sombrero, a long coat and buckskin breeches. He had a protruding paunch, and his cheeks were heavily jowled. The description is similar to that given an apparition that has been seen by others in the mountains near Pecos.

Fleeing from the phantom, the man who found the trove staggered through the dark, pursued by a persistent voice in the hills, moaning, "*No se este'! No se este'!*" ("Don't stay! Don't stay!"). Others have presumably heeded that warning. And should you ever proceed up a trackless arroyo as night falls in the area, listen for hoofbeats behind you.

The Town That Never Was

When driving along New Mexico Highway 44, don't stray far from the pavement, particularly to the west of La Ventana, lest you come upon the lights of a town that doesn't exist.

Many people in that neck of the Jemez Mountains have seen the town glimmering in the moonlight since it was first reported a number of years ago by a cowboy.

Riding out from the village of La Ventana to visit a ranch, the cowboy topped a rise and saw the lights of a sizeable community in the valley below. Curious because he knew of no towns or ranch houses in the vicinity, he entered the village. The streets were deserted.

He rode up to a house and rapped on the front door. When he did this, all the lights in the town suddenly went out. Frightened, the cowboy jumped on his horse and galloped away.

The next morning, the cowboy and a friend returned to the site. They found nothing but the crumbling adobe foundation of an old ranch house.

The mysterious town is situated near the fabled Ojo del Espiritu Santo ("Spring of the Holy Ghost"), which drew its name from a Spaniard who, while standing guard one night, saw two mist-like wraiths rise from the ground, practically paralyzing him with fright.

The Witch of Villagra's Hall

In the middle hours between dusk and dawn, the measured footsteps of the wandering witch of the Villagra building echo along a deserted hallway. Although the old building in the New Mexico Capitol complex has apparently been haunted for many years, state employees who work there (the building's tenants include divisions of the Game and Fish Department and the Veterans Service Commission) are loath to talk about it except among themselves.

One veteran worker, inclined to toil into the late hours, has, on more than one occasion, encountered the apparition. "I know some people don't believe it," the worker says, "but that's all right. It wasn't my imagination. I know what I saw."

The ghost appears as an old woman wearing a kerchief and a floor-length dress from the late eighteenth century. Curiously and inexplicably, a small lap dog rides on her shoulder. Pacing the corridor, she beckons with her finger for witnesses to follow and then vanishes through a wall.

A few hold the belief that the ghost is a woman who was beheaded as a witch at the site of the Villagra building. Since this seems contradictory to New Mexico culture, a second contention is more likely: the building is situated over an old, unmarked graveyard, and the ghost represents the kindred spirits of those whose final rest has been disturbed.

A ghost of a witch is said to haunt the halls of the Villagra building. *Wikimedia Commons.*

THE CHAMBERINO HORROR

Another strange story that was almost as wild as the tales from the north came from south of New Mexico. On the outskirts of Chamberino, a quiet village between Las Cruces and El Paso, there stands a 140-year-old adobe home, which includes an adjoining chapel. One night around 1:00 a.m., the young son of the family who had just moved in woke his parents in terror, continually screaming, "The man is going to get me! The man is going to get me!"

At first, the family tried to ignore the strange happenings in their new home. Later, when they met the previous owners—a family with whom they had never been acquainted—they discovered their young son had also slept in the same room and had woken his parents up around 1:00 a.m. often, screaming, "The man is going to get me!" This only increased the uneasiness of the situation.

Another family who had previously lived in the house had been forced to flee after being startled awake multiple times by mysterious noises, such as clanking buckets and shaking chains, books suddenly falling from their shelves for no apparent cause and items seemingly vanishing. In the middle of the night, the lights would switch on without explanation, and doors and windows would unlock.

The primary source of the house's terror has long been attributed to its previous owner. Rumor has it that a young man visited the old man who had lived there and abruptly disappeared under suspicious circumstances. Supposedly, one of the laborers working on the property stumbled on an underground room with nothing more than skeletal remains and a hollow wooden box inside. When he alerted his employer about what he found, he was immediately fired in a fit of rage.

Others believe that the four-foot-thick walls of the old chapel near the home hold the bodies of some nuns who were left alone when the locals rushed off to fight a group of Natives. The chapel wasn't finished when they left, but it was complete and empty when they returned. It is assumed that since the nuns' remains weren't laid to rest properly, they now haunt the site.

Nevertheless, if you sit and watch the fieldhands today, you will notice they make arduous detours to avoid the house.

The Face at the Window

If you're ever in Isleta on some windy and moonless night and you see a white dog, it would be wise to give it wide berth. It might be the spirit of a spurned lover, shot to death some fifty years ago.

At that time, a young and beautiful maiden so captured the heart and mind of a young Native that he repeatedly professed his passion for her. Yet she rejected him, and the Native was eventually ordered away by the girl's father.

One night, not long thereafter, the father entertained a visitor, a white man, in his home. Both men noticed the face of a motionless white dog in the window, whereupon the host remarked that the animal arrived every night to peer through the pane with weary and mournful eyes. Rising, he went outside and chased the dog away. This was repeated several times during the evening until the visitor resolved to remedy his friend's problem.

The next time the face of the white dog appeared in the window, the visitor went outside and, as the dog ran, shot it dead. The two men thought nothing more of it until the visitor rose to leave. Walking outside, they found the body of the young suitor precisely where the dog had fallen. The dog was gone—or so it seemed. There are nights, they say, when a white dog lopes through the darkness in Isleta, looking for his assailant or his lost love—or both.

2
CASA VIEJA

Nestled in the quaint farming community of Corrales is an establishment that has captured the essence of history through its decor and culture, Casa Vieja. The name is Spanish for "old house," and it was once the ancestral home of the esteemed Martinez family. The building has stood since the early 1700s, before the founding of the city of Albuquerque.

In 1710, Francisco Montey Vigil was granted a piece of land known as Alameda, which included the Corrales area. After a short time, he sold it to Captain Juan Gonzales. His sister's husband, Salvatore Martinez, purchased a portion of this grant for 250 cows and constructed a house in 1706 or 1712. This building served as an itinerant court until the Perea home was built. It was also the location of a cavalry encampment from Albuquerque and Santa Fe, who were dispatched to protect against Natives. It later became a stagecoach stop and grocery store owned by the Moretto family before being remodeled into its current form as a restaurant in the 1970s.

This house follows an E-shaped hacienda-style construction, with walls over thirty inches thick made of terrones adobe bricks. Inside the building, you can find wood details like hand-carved doors, roped frames around the windows and original vigas supporting the roof. The west end of this fifty-five-foot-long room is rumored to contain a chapel dedicated to Our Lady of the Conception, which Don Juan Gonzales built. The old walls also contain carvings, and odd objects like nickels have been found embedded within

Casa Vieja is one of the oldest buildings in Corrales. *Photograph by the author.*

them. All of these are believed to have been left by Alejandro Gonzales Baz's son Gaspar, who obtained permission from the Ordinary and Bishop Tamaron before their creation.

The first public statement of the supposed haunting of the building appeared in the *Albuquerque Journal* on July 8, 1987, in conjunction with an announcement that the building was on the market.

> *CORRALES—FOR SALE: an adobe pasta palace in the rustic downtown with an over 270-year legacy, buried treasure and a resident ghost.*
>
> *Sonya Bentley doesn't know how long Harold the Ghost, who was dubbed that by a waiter, has made the "J" dining room at Casa Vieja restaurant his "home."*
>
> *It could be that the spirit's been relighting extinguished candles since 1706 or 1712 when historians figure the cavernous structure was built. It was constructed by a relative of Capt. Juan Gonzales, who had bought the Corrales section of the Alameda Land Grant.*
>
> *Employees swear the ghost is there, and psychics say they've felt a presence in one dining room, Bentley asserts. But the building has had so many inhabitants it's hard to tell where Harold might have popped up from. In addition to being a residence the massive adobe has housed a chapel, a*

garrison of Spanish soldiers, a mental hospital, a hospital for tuberculosis patients, and just regular folks, too.

And there's also the legend about an ivory and gold statue of Our Lady of Guadalupe that is buried somewhere in the thick mud walls. A 16th-century Spanish sword was uncovered in one wall, and Bentley's son, Alec, who's now 21, used to tap on the walls In search of buried treasure.

The family home was the rear of the building for the first five or six years.

"It was great," Alec said. "I had the best time. I mean just tearing through the dining room with your pajamas on. Knock down your mother, terrorize the waiters, throw butter at them, throw vinegar, you know.…I was absolutely hated, but it was great."

When Chef Jim and his wife, Annette, began running the establishment in 1999, they quickly realized it was haunted. Even though they were doubtful of this fact, strange occurrences continually made them rethink their beliefs. Every night, they would lock up the building and activate the alarm. But when they returned in the morning, all the doors would be wide open, and the alarm had never gone off. How could the doors open without any sign of forced entry or setting off the alarm?

When the otherworldly events began taking place in the form of flickering lights and levitating margarita glasses, a call was put out for help. They hired a "professional ghost buster," who managed to send more than three hundred spirits back to the other world. Since then, the strange phenomena have been much less frequent, but not all of the ghosts have departed, and odd occurrences still take place.

People who have eaten in the restaurant tell tales of supernatural happenings. Karen and her husband, Doug, experienced one such occurrence when they went out for drinks and dinner with friends. Karen reported seeing something quite strange that night.

As my husband and I entered the lounge; my friend Julie and her boyfriend were the only people on that side of the room, and they called for us. I immediately noticed that there was a cloud of smoke over their table. The problem was that no one was smoking. It just hung over the table for a second and then went away. I jokingly made a comment about the smoke; however, neither of my friends or my husband had noticed it at all. I did not think much about it at first, but after a while, it became more curious. It looked more like a cloud than cigarette smoke. It was all massed together into a clump. What was that smoke? Where did it come from? Where did it go?

Other customers have also seen a mysterious Hispanic woman in a white dress seated on a bench near the fireplace in the lounge. She just sits there and smiles. While there is nothing unusual about that, this "woman" has a habit of vanishing from the room.

Jim White provided more information about the eerie past of the building in an interview that was printed in the *Albuquerque Journal*, dated February 5, 2005.

Most Albuquerque and Corrales residents probably know the Casa Vieja as an upscale restaurant. That's the identity it has carried for the past 30 years, although not under one owner. The well-known television chef Jim White has owned and cooked for the restaurant since 1999.

But the history of the Casa Vieja, literally translated from the Spanish as "the old house," goes back much further, more like 300 years.

It is thought to be one of the oldest buildings in Corrales, according to the book Corrales Historic Buildings *by the Village of Corrales Historic Preservation Committee.*

Some say the building was constructed around 1700 by Juan Gonzales for his daughter, but others date it after 1718, when Salvador Martinez bought the land it now sits on for up to 500 cows. Over the years, the Casa Vieja's size has ranged from four to 20 rooms; today it has 14, with seven working fireplaces and some rooms with 30-inch walls.

During its early years, the Casa Vieja at various times reportedly served as a stagecoach stop, a military headquarters for the Spanish, a courthouse, the headquarters for a cavalry unit, a tuberculosis clinic and a nudist colony.

White, in showing a visitor through his restaurant recently, said the building has its original vigas, and until several years ago still had gun turrets high on one wall of the oldest room, once a chapel.

Jim says when Casa Vieja was a courthouse, defendants would be tried there, and then marched down Corrales Road with bystanders throwing food and rocks at them. When they reached what is now the Rancho de Corrales restaurant, nearby, he says, justice would be meted out on the famous hanging tree there.

Today, White and his wife, Annette, say the past gets in their faces with a very active population of ghosts. At first they didn't believe in departed spirits showing themselves, but in the several years they have owned Casa Vieja, they have been convinced by a relentless series of crashing glasses and pitchers, carefully locked doors opening, plates that won't stay in front of diners, and even an unknown bar patron who disappears and reappears.

"For quite a while, we would lock up the restaurant at night and set the alarm, and time after time we would find the doors standing open the next day, without the alarm having been tripped," according to Annette.

"We finally arranged for a woman to come here and do a ghost-busting session because things were getting too crazy. Prayers were said, and after the session, things were 100 percent better."

Jim White says one spirit that stayed was that of a 7-foot-plus Hessian soldier, who had served at the Casa Vieja when it was a military outpost. "He was head of security and was killed here. He still believes he needs to protect the place."

Jim says people never see a ghost straight-on, but rather, out of the corners of their eyes. "Your mind doesn't filter peripheral vision," Jim says. "Usually, I'll just see the Hessian's boot clearing the doorway. He has huge feet, buckles on his boots and a gold medallion on one shoe."

A few of the spirits have been captured in photos, one of them a group shot which also shows a white shape that no one saw when the picture was taken. The photo now hangs in a prominent place in the restaurant.

These days the Whites are busy with a brisk business at the Casa Vieja and have come to treat their ghosts as a normal part of running a business in a 300-year-old building—perhaps even a bonus. One of them is the ghost of a Corrales politician who the Whites have been told is determined to help keep the Casa Vieja successful.

In 2021, I was a part of T.J. Trout's ghost hunt for 96.3 KKOB radio. We spoke with the current owners, Gary and Linda Socha, about the history and ghostly activity of the building.

Mr. Martinez came here with an Alameda land grant in his pocket, and he decided to build a house. This house was actually built for his daughter. She lived here, and it stayed in the Martinez family until 1942.

During that time of 1770 to 1942, it was a number of things. It was certainly a residence for the family, but in those times, you have to understand that it had to be a number of things. For instance, it was a courthouse for a while. So, they would have trials here on a Saturday afternoon they would move all the furniture out of the main room, and they would have what amounted to a trial, a judge trial. If you were convicted, they would take you out on Corrales Road and march you down the road, where you would be pelted with rotten vegetables until you arrived at the territorial house where they had the hanging tree.

French nuns lived here in the past, and soldiers were housed here long ago. *Photograph by the author.*

So, this was the courthouse, and that was the punishment. French nuns lived here for a while, and soldiers were housed here once upon a time. It was also a general store, and we know it was all of these things until 1942, when it left the family and was purchased by Mrs. Harrington. The building was starting to collapse at that time. We actually have some photos of it, and it has twenty rooms.

There were really only three rooms standing, so a major remodel brought it back to its original glory, and the Harringtons lived in it until 1970. And at that time, it was transformed into another residence. It was also a psychiatric hospital for a while. There was a therapy pool that was in the back, and after that, it was a high-end restaurant for fifty years. A fun story is that forty-two years ago, Lynn and I were having a margarita in the bar on our honeymoon. We had rifled through the couch to find change so that we could afford that margarita. But we eventually bought the place, which somehow makes sense. I'm not quite sure how that worked, but it did make sense.

So, over the years, it was a lot of different things. The thing that we love about it—this is obviously our…our passion project—is that everybody has a Casa Viejas story. You know, it can be a ghost story. It could be we got married there, it could be our wedding reception was there. But everybody has a story, and we have a lot of fun doing what we do, and people really like coming here and hanging out and drinking some beverages and listening to music.

Next, Gary's wife, Linda, told us about some of her supernatural encounters in the old building.

I approached the building with the idea that I thought it would be fun if it was haunted, but I didn't have any idea whether it was or not. One day shortly after we bought it, I was here cleaning up Christmas decorations after Christmas, and I was here by myself during the day, and I heard all of this commotion going on like somebody came in the back door and walked through the kitchen as if they were carrying shopping bags or something. I mean, you know that sound, that bustling sound of somebody walking through. And I immediately assumed it was Gary. And because he was popping in and out with during the construction and stuff—well, as it turns out, it wasn't Gary. There was no one here but me. And that was pretty…it really freaked me out in the beginning, and I was kind of afraid to be here by myself.

But over time, I've learned that we have Casper the friendly ghost here, and the things that consistently happen are doors opening and closing. The first time it happened was with one of our electricians. He went into this closet over there to add an outlet. Soon after that, I heard all this screaming and thumping and banging, and I ran in there, and the door closed behind him, latching him in. It's always in the same place in the building.

Since then, Gary has been working on the heating. He's been kind of a skeptic. And he was working on the heating one day on a ladder right in that hallway, and the bathroom door opened right behind him all by itself. And, you know, being an engineer, he figured, "Oh, there's got to be an air current or something." He tried to recreate it, and he couldn't. Then he called me, and he said, "You know, maybe there's something to this ghost thing."

I've also been on the patio when the door would just open and close all by itself. Just last week, one of our servers walked into the back part of the building, and a spring-loaded door that stays closed all the time opened in front of her as she walked up to it. She just like, "Well, and that's it." The

For the most part, the ghosts that haunt Casa Vieja are friendly. *Photograph by the author.*

thing is, you never…there's no way to anticipate it. You never know when it's going to happen. It's just crazy.

It probably took a couple of years to accept it. We've had other ghost investigations here, and I've learned a little more about it. And every report from anyone that I trust says consistently there's nothing negative here—it's positive. The previous owner talked about seeing a ghost, and we really didn't know much more than that. It was a colonel with epaulets on his shoulder, which, ironically, is something we've never had any experience with, and I'm not sure he didn't say that to boost the sale ability of the property.

Linda then related a tale that was published in the *Albuquerque Journal* on November 25, 2018.

The walls would know if it's true that the bodies of two monks were once discovered buried within them. The walls could tell us how the portrait of a 17th-century French duke came to be secreted in another of Casa Vieja's partitions.

"An adobe contractor found the painting in a wall that had water damage," said Gary Socha, who, with his wife, Linda, and daughter, Maria Socha, own Casa Vieja and have operated it as an event center since 2016.

23

The duke's portrait was water-logged and mud-covered.

"It had three holes in it," Gary said.

Refurbished and reframed by Santa Fe art restorer Linda Nader, the painting of the duke, since identified as Jean Louis de Nogaret de La Valette (1554–1642), now hangs on one of those silent Casa Vieja walls.

Even though the portrait's presence at Casa Vieja remains a mystery, it plays a role in the ever-evolving epic of the old house. The oil portrait of the duke, which now hangs in Casa Vieja's Sunroom, is believed to have been painted in Spain in the 1600s. Duke Nogaret de La Valette was an influential member of the French nobility and was awarded the titles of Admiral of France and Governor of Normandy, among others. He was involved in politics and plots throughout his life and was eventually exiled after striking a powerful rival in a public altercation.

The presence of his portrait inside a wall of Casa Vieja is part of the building's mystique—like the story of the two monks, wearing robes, crosses and folded hands on their chests, said to have been found interred in one of the building's interior walls.

Linda Socha said they were told where the monks' remains had been sent, but there is no record of their bones at that place. Only the walls know the truth.

Linda elaborated on the story of the hidden portrait during my visit there in 2021.

It was quite common for them to do things like that because, actually, there were two little windows above the fireplace in the other room where they shot, you know, watched for enemies and shot out the windows. And I mean this, at one point in time, this was a hostile area, and they were worried about that, so they would hide things so they wouldn't be stolen.

We had a wonderful art show in the building, a tribute show, and this is when this happened. And this room in the building tends to be more consistent as well. It's in the very back. We used to call it the library. It's one of the older rooms, not the oldest. So, I'm helping this guy hang this art show. He's…he's been hired by Weems [Gallery and Framing] *to hang the show professionally. I'm outside gardening, and I come in from a bright sunny day and walk into the backroom. It's kind of dark. I look to the one side, and I see through the doorway of a very sunny room a shadow. And my first thought was, "Well, why is the Weems guy way back here when he was working up in the front of the building?"*

The painting of the duke, who has since been identified as Jean Louis de Nogaret de La Valette (1554–1642). *Photograph by the author.*

So, I stopped and took off my glasses and walked around the corner, and as I do, I see a foot, as if someone was walking away from you and all you caught was the very remnant if they were going through a door. It was a foot and ankle in the trousers. I was able to go online and figure out the time frame based on the shoe. It looked like a military shoe and some type of uniform—a khaki green pant leg and a brown shoe from the 1930s. At the same time, I saw a shadow over my head like a flock of geese had flown over. But I was inside. So, it happened so quickly, and for the longest time, I thought about it. I can't get the imprint out of my head.

Well, I went running up to the front of the building, and I asked the guy that was up on the ladder, "Did you just come in the backroom?" I still couldn't believe I'd seen it. He said, "No, I've been right here." I asked if he had an assistant or a friend. "No," he said. "Just us."

Gary was kind enough to speak in more detail about the monks who were rumored to have been buried inside the walls.

Well, it's a little bit of a believable story in that something that a lot of people don't realize is that Corrales originally flooded every year because there weren't any levees between here and the river. So, it would flood every year. And as a matter of fact, a lot of the buildings would be washed away and the vigas would go down to the river, and they would go down, pick up the vigas, come back and build your building back. So, one of the things that became popular, like the old church here in Corrales, they were tired of losing their cemetery to the floods. So, they built a stone foundation box essentially, and they buried people underneath the floors of the church. So, it's not that far of a stretch to say, "Let's put them in the walls to keep them from floating away." So, that's the only explanation I've heard that seems to be plausible.

Another fun story occurred when an artist came up to me and asked, "OK, so what's the deal with the keystone?"

I replied, "I don't know what you mean."

"Well, look at the floor. Do you ever vacuum the floor and mop the floor?"

"Well, you know, about ten thousand times."

"Well, haven't you ever noticed?"

"Notice what?"

"The keystone."

Again, I replied, "No."

So, he took me into what we call the chapel and he said, "See how all of these little stones are angular little square stones?"

There's basically a three-foot stone, which is a hell of a big stone, and it's shaped like a keystone. And I look at it, and I go, "Wow, that's incredible. It seems to be pointing over to that wall. What are you thinking?"

"I'm thinking we're going to make some money. We're going to do a reality show—the lifting of the stone. You know, if Geraldo can do it with the vault and there was nothing in it, we can do it with the stone."

I looked at it and said, "You know, is it just me or does that kind of look like a little tiny coffin? No, we're not doing that. We're leaving it right there." But I said, "It does point over to there."

And he said, "I've been told there's a golden Madonna in the wall somewhere. And so, maybe it's…it's pointing to that."

"Well, I…I'll tell you what I know for sure is that I've cut into these walls quite often. And when I cut into them, money gets sucked in, and I've never seen any gold fall out. So, that's what I know for sure."

3

THE LUNA MANSION

Nestled in the lush, green valley, Los Lunas is a quaint town with a population of twenty thousand. The gentle murmur of the Rio Grande River serves as a natural soundtrack to life here, its waters carving a path through the landscape. Horses are still used for transportation, and life moves slower here than elsewhere. The town honors its past, and one remnant of this is the Luna-Otero Mansion, which was built before the railroad connected distant parts of the country. This estate is associated with two powerful Spanish families who reigned over Los Lunas many years ago.

In 1692, the Lunas and Oteros arrived in New Mexico, with Domingo de Luna leading the Lunas family and Don Pedro Otero heading the Otero clan. As time passed, the two families amassed great wealth from their land and livestock holdings. They soon became prominent in both social and political realms. As was a common practice among affluent families, the two joined forces when Solomon Luna married Adelaida Otero and Manuel Otero wed Eloisa Luna. Together, they created a powerful dynasty, forcing the Santa Fe Railroad to comply with their demands.

In 1880, the Santa Fe Railroad was creeping through New Mexico. The engineering plans it had in place meant the railroad would run through Luna territory. The railroad had to negotiate with the Lunas to gain access to that land. Eventually, a deal was made that promised the construction of a magnificent home, built specifically for Don Antonio Jose Luna and his family's preferences, as payment for the right-of-way. Don Antonio had explored numerous areas in the South. He desired a house that mirrored those grandiose architectural designs he'd seen while visiting different plantations. As such, the railroad constructed a stately mansion in the Southern colonial style, using adobe as the home's primary material.

Don Antonio barely had the chance to enjoy his new home before he died in it a year later. The mansion was then passed on to his oldest son, Tranquilino. Still, while working for the Senate in Washington, D.C., he, too, became sick. He perished, leaving the house to his younger brother Solomon Lunas. When he passed away in the early twentieth century, his nephew Eduardo Otero and his wife, Josefita Manderfield Otero, inherited the property.

Josefita Otero, or "Pepe" as she was affectionately known, was greatly admired in Los Lunas and beyond. She spent her days tending to her gardens and painting, often donating her time and financial contributions to worthy efforts that served the community. The Luna-Otero Mansion grew even more luxurious under Josefita's care. She added a solarium, portico and decorative ironwork, which gave the house a royal look. Most of these additions have been maintained, minus some scaling back of the ironwork. Even today, the mansion stands resplendent in its former glory.

The Luna-Oteros were the last two residents of the mansion before it was bought by Eunice Sullivan, who lived there with her sons for several years. In 1975, she petitioned to have the property listed in the National Register of Historic Places. This caught the attention of Earl Whittemore, a preservationist who then purchased the estate with his associates, converting it into an upscale restaurant in 1978. More ghost stories about the mansion would soon follow. However, they predate the restaurant. The oldest newspaper article about these stories appeared on October 30, 1975, while the mansion was being restored.

Are there "ghosts" in the Luna Mansion? There are likely to be Friday night. That's when the Mansion will be open for short tours for children age 12 and under. The tours will be conducted from 6–9 p.m. and there will be no charge for children, providing groups of eight children or less are accompanied by a paid adult. Each tour will last 15–20 minutes and groups will be conducted through the mansion one at a time, so there may be a brief waiting period, and while touring the mansion, the children will discover whether or not there are really ghosts there.

After this article, another did not appear in the papers until the *Albuquerque Journal* published the following on February 23, 1991.

The Luna Mansion in 1946. *Library of Congress.*

*On slow nights at the Luna Mansion—a popular Los Lunas restaurant—
it is said Josefita Otero swirls proudly through the grand house she loved
and made so charmingly beautiful.*

*"Everything that this house became is because of Josefita," restaurant
manager David Scovill says.*

*Josefita, or "Pepe," is dead, but Scovill and other employees of the
restaurant insist Pepe still haunts the magnificent southern plantation style
adobe that has graced Los Lunas since 1881.*

*Bartender Jeanette Blaylock says she has seen the fastidious, artistic
woman whose murals and original paintings still adorn the restaurant's
walls. Recounting her sightings of Pepe, Blaylock is sincere. There is no
tongue in cheek in her descriptions. And other employees report unexplained
phenomena, like moving cocktail glasses, lights that go back on after they've
been turned off, dead-bolted doors that come open and unscrewed lightbulbs.*

*"Pepe made this house so beautiful that we assumed she just didn't
want to leave it," Blaylock says. She notes Josefita supervised much of
the 1920s remodeling, which saw the addition of the solarium, the front
portico, and the ironwork which surrounds the building. Josefita and her
husband moved into the house in 1912 and lived there about 20 years. She
died in California.*

Pepe also painted the solarium's murals of a peasant woman balancing a bowl of fruit on her head and of two singing Mexican mariachis. A large oil painting as she saw herself—a shepherd girl tending her sheep— dominates the main dining area that looks out a north bay window.

Blaylock has worked at the mansion for five years. She says most of her sightings of Pepe happened on the second floor, former bedrooms that now make up the lounge. The restaurant opened in 1977 after the house had stood vacant for several years, Scovill says.

Blaylock says Pepe seemed to be most active soon after the restaurant opened.

"We assume she just wasn't used to people going in and out of her home," Blaylock says. "I don't think she liked that idea."

Blaylock says she has seen the ghost several times. "Usually, what I see is a little old lady walking around here in a long black dress, and it's usually just for a second out of the corner of my eye, and usually when I'm alone."

In the southeast corner of the upper room at the top of the stairs, an antique rocking chair sits next to a grandfather clock and decorative body-length mirror. It's here Pepe sits and greets visitors, it is said.

At the bottom of the stairs, Pepe's black and white portrait hangs on a wall in the main entrance hallway, next to the photographs of other important Los Lunas residents of the early 1900s. Her wavy black hair is combed up, crowning an attractive, but not beautiful, face. She wears a white blouse with a lace bodice and no jewelry. Her pensive, mysterious eyes gaze thoughtfully out over the room.

Last summer, descendants of the Otero family, the Los Lunas dynasty that once owned the home, got together for a reunion at the mansion. Scovill says one of Pepe's daughters told him a story about a time when Pepe herself encountered two ghosts in the house. Sometime after her husband, Eduardo, died, Pepe was in the upstairs bedroom early one morning when she heard talking downstairs, the story goes. Thinking her servants—Compadre Cruz and Maria the maid—were downstairs, she called down and asked to be served coffee. She looked down and saw a man and a woman.

When the servants failed to bring her coffee, she called out again. Still no response. A third time, she called out for coffee. Angry and frustrated, Pepe rushed downstairs to upbraid the servants, but found the house deserted and all the doors locked. She rushed to Compadre Cruz's living quarters out on the grounds and found the servant bedridden with the flu. She then found a note from Maria, telling Pepe she had to go to Belen to care for her sick mother.

The exterior of the Luna Mansion in 2000. *Photograph by the author.*

Realizing the people she saw must have been ghosts, according to the story, the haughty grand lady snorted unimpressed, "Maybe they were ghosts, but they were obviously only of servant class!"

Blaylock says she also may have seen one of the servant ghosts.

"I was in the storeroom stocking beer when I turned around and I saw a man walk through an adobe wall through some chicken wire mesh and then into the other wall," Blaylock says. "At first I thought it was just a busboy, but then I realized busboys don't come walking out of walls and disappear."

"Man, I tell you I jumped down those stairs and it took me a long time to want to come up here again, and I wouldn't come up alone," she says. There are still some employees who won't go up to the second floor alone after dark, she adds.

For a time, Pepe's rocking chair was kept in the storeroom, but employees say they saw it rocking or heard strange creaks. They thought Pepe wanted her chair in its customary place at the top of the stairs, and so it was returned there.

Also, Blaylock says the chair never gathers dust on the armrests or on the seat, where Pepe is believed to sit. There have been other strange occurrences: A wine glass exploded. A picture of Salomon Luna, one of the original occupants, posing with President William Howard Taft floated off the wall and then back. Cocktail glasses have tipped over or moved. A wine cellar door that was dead-bolted shut was opened, setting off an alarm. An image appeared in a storeroom mirror, and then disappeared. Lights that have been shut off come back on. Lightbulbs have been unscrewed. Some customers have reported feeling a cold chill or having the backs of their heads touched.

"These ghosts feel like this is their home and they show up when they want to," Scovill says.

The ghost stories charm most customers, although they frighten some, Scovill says. "I don't know how the ghosts feel about sharing this place with us, but they never get in the way," Scovill says. "It's like they're saying, 'Hey, we're here so you better get used to us.'"

In September 2000, I visited the mansion and was able to speak with David Scoville about some of the other supernatural encounters he had while working at the restaurant.

The storeroom on the second floor, where Pepe's rocking chair was stored. *Photograph by the author.*

I began working at the Luna Mansion in 1979 and was a kitchen manager until 1983. After a three-year hiatus, I returned and took on the role of general manager/owner. I have plenty of knowledge about the mansion's past and all the stories about its resident spirits. The building was commissioned by the railroad for the Luna/Otero family between 1878 and 1881 with a price tag of $47,000. It is a two-story adobe structure built in the Victorian/Southern style.

My first recollection of an apparition happened in the year 1980, between midnight and one in the morning. I was upstairs in the mansion, tending to my bartending duties: I was making sure that all the patrons had left, inspecting rooms for any cigarette butts or debris they may have littered behind. The room is furnished with gorgeous antiques—chairs, sofas and tables—so at the end of every shift, we make sure to check if anything has been damaged, like cigarette burns. Most importantly, we scan for smoldering ashes or cigarettes; a fire could easily start in such an old house.

I was making my rounds in the northeast room when I noticed an Art Deco lamp with a fringe ribbon around its shade, moving out of the corner of my eye. Thinking that perhaps an employee had neglected to turn off the air conditioner, I reached to feel if there was any cold air coming from the vent. But there wasn't any, so I realized it must be off. As I turned around, I spotted the fabric swaying again.

The shadows of the fringe appeared to move around the shape of the lamp, and then an image of Josefita—the original owner of the house—came into view. Josefita was known for painting murals and artwork throughout this abode. She seemed to be tracing her finger around the base of the lamp; she wore a plain white clothing ensemble that I assume women dressed in during the 1920s. Without taking any time to think, I ran down the stairs and out of the front door, not even bothering to switch off lights or close registers. I was scared and out of breath, with my hair standing up on end as if I had been struck with a physical blow. All I can remember about her is that she had no jewelry, her hair was tied up in a bun and she donned a long white skirt.

Josefita did not have a see-through body, like some people might expect from a ghost. She was as solid and real as any person. Due to my fear, I couldn't even remember her facial expression—whether she smiled or frowned or something else entirely. As I stood near the entrance gate, I cast my gaze up to the second-floor window and saw her still standing there, looking at me.

The Art Deco lamp was located near the small table (*lower left*). This is where David saw the apparition of Josefita. *Photograph by the author.*

I have since discovered that the upstairs barroom is Josefita's favorite haunt, the place where she most often appears. The barroom was once her master bedroom, and many employees and patrons have experienced various phenomena, such as goosebumps, cold chills, breathlessness and sensing her presence. It turns out that they are actually seeing her, just like I did. After reading about the history of Luna Mansion, I learned that Josefita's bedroom used to be located at the northwest corner of the house. However, after her husband died, she relocated to the northeast corner.

It is also believed that Josefita appears or makes her presence known at the top of the staircase leading to the bar on the second floor. This was the spot where she had a heart attack.

My second experience took place at about 10:00 a.m. in that very spot. As I was making my way upstairs with two cases of beer at around ten in the morning, I noticed a woman walking from the bar's newly built cocktail station to the northeast room. Assuming it was Susie, our housekeeper, I called out, "Hi, Susie!" But soon after entering the attic storeroom, I realized that it wasn't Susie but Josefita. Her dress and her tightly pinned hair were exactly as they had been when she was alive. The sight took me by surprise, and I dropped the beer, stumbled down the stairs and quickly left. Later on, when discussing my experience with her descendants, they confirmed that it must have been Josefita—every detail matched perfectly to how she used to look.

One evening, while strolling outside the house, I thought I felt someone watching me. I dismissed the feeling until it became unbearable. Then, peering up to the mansion's second floor, I saw Josefita wearing her white dress, eyes fixed on me. There are other strange things going on in the mansion. Lightbulbs suddenly unscrew themselves for no reason and can dependably be found detached each night.

As I roam the halls of the mansion, I can already predict which light fixtures will have their bulbs unscrewed in the morning. The grandiose chandeliers in the main dining room consistently draw the attention of our resident specter, while other lights around the house are tampered with as well. No matter the source, however, the chandeliers remain its favorite.

The stairs leading down from the second floor of the mansion. *Photograph by the author.*

I remember a particular night in December 1987. A female guest was having dinner with a male friend, her sister and three children. We welcomed them into our dining room, seating the man who had a ponytail by the entrance. Everyone went through their meal without problems until I was asked to come to their table by the host. As a manager in the restaurant, I had to attend to any questions or issues that customers might have. When I approached their table, I noticed that all of them were completely motionless.

The man voiced his shock, saying that someone had yanked and tugged at his ponytail. But with a quick glance around, he could see no one nearby who could have done it. Everyone else present saw the sudden movement of his hair but nothing more—no one seemed to have noticed anyone actually pulling it. As he finished describing what had happened, suddenly, all the light bulbs in the chandelier above us exploded as if they were being struck by shots from a BB gun. Glass rained down onto the people and their meals. We all covered our eyes from the shards with our hands and napkins. After just a few seconds, everything was quiet again. I expressed my apologies and told them we would replace their dinners. Surprisingly, they stayed for the rest of the evening. The staff quickly brought ladders and replaced the broken bulbs with new ones.

An old, antique table owned by the Manderfield family and said to be three centuries old is still in their possession. It's a large table that can seat fifteen people comfortably and is only reserved for special occasions—parties, dinners, etc. Although it is beautiful, this table has some eerie secrets of its own. I was helping to set the table up with flatware and decorations when, all of a sudden, I noticed something amiss. After we set out the glasses, they began to shatter uncontrollably across the dining room floor. Besides this strange phenomenon, other weird occurrences took place; huge double doors leading into the kitchen opened of their own accord, and water faucets switched on without warning. Ever since then, we've had to expect the unexpected whenever the Manderfield table is brought into the mansion.

In 1980, I hired Birdie Tapia as a bartender. Birdie's encounter with the ghost of Josefita in the second-floor attic was an experience she'll never forget. She said that when she opened the door to get supplies, the room was filled with light, and her eyes were drawn to the rocking chair where Josefita sat. Immediately, she ran away! Since then, the rocker has been moved from the storage area to the stair landing on the second floor.

On October 30, 2000, other employees shared their experiences with the *Albuquerque Tribune*.

"I've talked to a ghost," Devyn Scovill, David's 11-year-old daughter, said matter-of-factly. "I know it was a ghost. I know it was Josefita."

On a day earlier this week, Devyn, holding the clarinet she is learning to play this year, was sitting downstairs in the mansion, in a room between the kitchen and the main dining room.

"I was practically raised here," she said. "One time my dad was having a meeting here, and I was upstairs watching cartoons. I was about 3 years old. This lady was watching TV with me. After a while, the lady said she was tired of watching cartoons and wanted to read me a book."

Devyn said she went downstairs to ask her father for a book.

"I told him that Josefita wanted to read to me," she said.

That sent David Scovill racing up the stairs. He found no one there.

"All he could tell me," Devyn said, "was that she must have gone out the back door. I don't go upstairs anymore."

Scovill believes his daughter had been visiting with Pepe's ghost.

"I had told Devyn about Josefita, but I never taught her that name. I taught her Pepe," he said. "There was no way she should have known the name Josefita back then, but that's who she said wanted to read to her."

The upstairs bar was where Josefita's bedroom was once located. Some say it is the most haunted spot in the building. *Photograph by the author.*

Strange things have been reported in the mansion since it became a restaurant more than 20 years ago—glasses that appear to move on their own, lights that turn on without human assistance, diners touched from behind by invisible hands.

"I hear conversations upstairs when no one is there," said Jessica Chavez, who does office work for the restaurant as well as occasional waitressing. "But just as soon as I realize there's talking, it stops."

And then there's the rocking chair at the top of the stairs next to the grandfather clock. It is reputed to have been Pepe's chair, and restaurant employees claim that it never gathers dust on its seat or armrests—like someone is sitting in it regularly.

Scovill said he has seen Pepe, a woman in a white blouse or white dress, more than once.

"I have had six or seven real clear sightings of ghosts over the years," he said. "Last spring, I saw a man about five foot, five, and wearing a brown, flat-brimmed farmer's hat walking through the business office area. I think that was Cruz, Pepe's servant."

And just a few weeks ago, at about 2 or 3 o'clock in the afternoon, Scovill watched from the kitchen as a woman dressed in blue walked past the staircase, went into the front dining room and disappeared.

"I think she had been one of the servants, too," Scovill said. "Steve Garcia, one of my main cooks, sees her a lot. I kid him about having a thing with her."

Scovill can kid about the ghosts. He said he has never been scared in the mansion. But late at night, when he's alone and locking up and the tips of his fingers start to tingle, he knows better than to look at the top of the stairs."

4

THE MINESHAFT TAVERN

Coal Gulch is nestled within the Ortiz Mountains, a rugged and formidable landscape between Albuquerque and Santa Fe. This narrow canyon was home to an abundance of coal, coveted by many for its energy-producing properties. As word of this rich resource traveled, the once-quiet gulch transformed into a bustling town known as Madrid. People from far-off places like Kansas and Pennsylvania flocked to its location in search of work in the booming coal industry. For years, the town hummed with activity as miners toiled away, generating millions of kilowatts of power and bringing home a steady income. But tragedy struck in 1932 when an explosion at the Morgan Jones Mine claimed the lives of thirteen miners, leaving a somber reminder of the dangers that came with this lucrative profession. The *Albuquerque Journal* recorded the tragic accident on December 8, 1932.

> *The bodies of 13 men killed in an explosion in the Morgan Jones mine about 8 o'clock Wednesday morning, were brought to the surface at 6 o'clock Wednesday evening, The fourteenth victim had been removed soon after the explosion. All of the 53 men in the mine had been accounted for. Six men were injured, none seriously.*
>
> *Several hundred persons were grouped around the entrance of the mine when the bodies were brought out by the rescue crews. Campfires were burning on the hillsides to furnish warmth to the watchers, presenting a grim picture.*

As the stretcher bearers, each with his miner's lantern on his cap, loaded the bodies heavily covered with blankets onto waiting open trucks, watchers waiting on the hillsides followed the procession about a mile into Madrid.

The bodies were taken to the hospital of the Albuquerque and Cerrillos company, where again several hundred persons, including many of the wives, children and relatives of the dead miners, were waiting.

A few hours after the first report of the explosion, a checkup revealed that 14 men were missing and their names were determined by others who were in the mine at the time of the explosion, but who escaped alive.

But until the bodies were removed, relatives had not entirely given up hope. They did not rush to the trucks on which the bodies were placed, but stoically, they followed the funeral cortege of the five rough trucks to the company hospital, converted into a morgue for the occasion.

The dead:

Bony Gabaldon, 37.
Augustine Padilla, 38.
Angel Ortiz, 34.
Guadalupe Morales, 23.
Pablo Escarino, 32.
Julien Ynostraza, 34.
Manuel Cabera, 24.
Telesfor Macias, 30.
Damacio Perez, 44.
Julien Garcia, 45.
Juan Acosta, 40.
Francisco Torejo, 25.
Batzar Oaxaca, 40.
Fusebio Ramos, 21.

All were married men, with the exception of Ramos.

At the hospital, the bodies were laid out in rows, and each miner's identification tag was placed upon him. Then widows and children ranging from youths attending high school in Cerrillos or Santa Fe to little tots who had been kept in the Madrid grade school all day as teachers tried to soften news of the tragedy, received the final fateful news as some relative turned back the dirty blanket and verified the identification tag placed upon it.

Six men were brought in from the mine in the forenoon, suffering from shock and suffocation from the smoke and dust. They were treated at the hospital by Dr. A.R. Causer and returned to their home.

These men were Jimmy Taylor, Rosalio Liscano, Guadalupe Saldivar, Rafael Juarez, Andrew Samiripa, and his son, Pete.

The cause of the explosion has not been determined by Warren Bracewell, state mine inspector, who rushed to the mine from Albuquerque, entered it shortly before noon, and assisted Superintendent Oscar Huber in the rescue work.

The explosion came before some of the miners reached their positions. The dead were found, many with their lunch pails in their hands. Others had not yet even taken off their coats to begin work.

Little debris fell as the result of the explosion and although three of the bodies were burned slightly, none was mangled. As the usual flame of a coal mine explosion swept down the passageways of the first and second dips of the fourth right entry, nearly three miles from the mine entrance, all of the oxygen in the area was consumed, and the men suffocated.

Bracewell said that some of the men apparently fell to the ground after having run a short distance in the direction of the main passageway. Others fell where they stood, caught either by "mine damp" or poisonous carbon monoxide gas.

The force of the air wave that precedes the flame and gas of such explosions jarred loose the safety devices such as rock dust barriers and heavy cloth curtains. These prevented the spread of the explosion and poisonous gas to other parts of the mine and probably saved the lives of the other miners at work.

At the time of the explosion, the men were working in the fourth right gallery, nearly three miles inside the mine. Gabaldon, Padilla and Ortiz were at the north end of the gallery, Morales at the hoist at the mouth of Number Two dip and the ten men were in Number Two dip.

A few hundred feet further down the gallery in Number One dip, another crew of men were at work. They escaped without injury other than shock.

The ten men so long missing were working under Juan Acosta, one of the ten who had sub-leased the Number Two dip from the company.

Following the first impact of the explosion, some ten men near the outer edge of the area made a dash for the main passageway. Three of these, including Jimmie Taylor, 19, son of H.L. Taylor, assistant superintendent of the company's Madrid mines, were overcome. They were picked up and carried out safely by their comrades.

Andres Sampria, rushing out, picked up an unconscious body and carried it with him. When he had reached the area of clear air, he learned that it was his own son Pete he had rescued.

The oxygen-helmeted rescuers, rushing back into the danger area, first stumbled upon the body of Guadalupe Morales, 22. He had made a dash for safety but fell just short of the rock dust barrier and his goal. His body was the only one to be removed from the mine in the forenoon.

The rescue work proceeded slowly. There were six oxygen helmets in the mine, and men equipped with these rushed into the area where the explosion occurred to see if some comrade was still alive. They located most of the bodies before noon, and four were removed to the clear air of the central passageway, but all were dead.

The ventilating system in the area was little damaged by the explosion, and was easily restored, members of the rescue parties said. It was not until the area had been ventilated and the bad air flushed out, that the remaining bodies were removed to the main passageway. They were hauled on rail cars to a spot near the main entrance and then the slow procession of stretcher bearers to the waiting trucks began.

For decades, a local tavern was a gathering place for miners and their families until it burned down on Christmas Day 1944, but it was rebuilt by

The Mineshaft Tavern is rumored to be haunted by several ghosts. *Photograph by the author.*

Oscar Joseph Huber, a stern man who ran the town for decades with vision and compassion. The new tavern was named The Mine Shaft Tavern, and when it opened in 1947, it boasted the longest stand-up bar in New Mexico. Forty feet long, the bar was where fatigued miners could prop themselves up after a long day spent doubled over in the mines.

By the mid-1950s, however, the coal industry had given way to natural gas. Madrid's economy quickly collapsed, rendering it a ghost town.

When Joe Huber, the original owner's son, began renting abandoned cabins to artists and hippies in the 1970s, Madrid suddenly came alive again. This small, historic town now boasts a unique character with its own tragedies tucked away in the past. Could the long-lost emotions of those who lived centuries ago still have a hold on this place? Could they be influencing the living today?

At the Mine Shaft Tavern, bartenders and customers have seen glasses fly off the bar and suddenly break on their own. Although the times of these experiences vary, they most often occur after 10:00 p.m. Doors are also known to open and swing back and forth on their own.

After hours, objects are mysteriously moved about, and sounds can be heard coming from the adobe walls, particularly in the small room on the north side of the building. Several apparitions have also been seen throughout the historic building. The most disturbing occurs when people look into mirrors and, instead of seeing their own reflection, see that of a ghost. Another apparition has been spotted on numerous occasions near the stage area. The ghost appears to be a woman wearing a long dress, but the sightings are often very short, no more than a few seconds in length.

The most commonly reported paranormal sighting is that of an odd spirit that has made an unexpected home in the restroom. The "restroom ghost" is known to be quite irritable. She prods customers from behind as they walk by. Some women report a feeling of being strangled when passing through the hallway that leads to the restroom. On certain occasions, the apparition has been seen entering the kitchen area, smashing dishes and then turning the lights on and off in the bar. When the restaurant shuts for the night, even the cleaning person who tidies up the bathrooms feels an ethereal presence.

People usually react strongly when they experience the ghost in the restroom. Many agree that this spirit is likely the soul of a young woman who lost her life in a catastrophic car accident right outside the bar. The phantom appears and speaks in the bathroom, and sometimes, a female form materializes out of one of the stalls before it vanishes into nothingness.

One diner had a truly frightful time in the restroom. She entered alone, only to glimpse the ghost's face when she looked into the mirror. Knowing full well that this eatery was haunted and having seen the ghost firsthand, the customer rushed out of the restroom in fear. Who could blame her for being so scared?

Another former employee recalled the encounters he had with the spirits of the tavern while he worked there as a bartender.

At first, I would be finishing up my shift at the bar around 3:00 a.m., when, out of the corner of my eye, I'd spot something. Tired and exhausted, I thought it was just my imagination playing tricks on me. While wrapping things up with one of my coworkers, I turned off all the lights in the building. We stopped by the bathroom to turn that light off as well. Suddenly, the bulb flickered and lit up again before darkening for good. My coworker and I ran out of there as fast as we could! The next night, he saw a looming shadow along the wall, even though no lights were on, adding to our hysteria.

One evening, I spotted a lovely customer across the room. She was there with her boyfriend, and they were the only people on that side of the bar. They called me over for drinks, but as I approached their table, I noticed something strange. A cloud of smoke hung over them, but no one in the vicinity smoked. The mysterious smoke hovered just for a second before vanishing into thin air.

Another night, I was bartending and talking to a guest about the hauntings in town. I told him there wasn't any ghost bothering me. Then, out of nowhere, I felt freezing cold. My eyes started watering with my eyelids fluttering uncontrollably, like my eyeballs wanted to roll back into my head. My hands started shaking, and I could hardly see straight. My friend walked up and asked if I was all right. But before I could answer, the feeling vanished, and I just felt cold for a moment. Every time I enter the corner of the tavern where things happen, my arm hair stands on end, and fear overwhelms me.

However, the haunting here is not just visible to those inside the tavern. I was sent an e-mail in which a young man described an "encounter" he had while walking by the place.

The sky was cloudless, and it was utterly calm and still, without even the slightest gust of wind. My fiancée and I had stopped in Madrid on the way

The tavern's stage and ladies' restroom have many terrifying tales associated with them. *Photograph by the author.*

to Santa Fe and wandered about the town, peering into stores and checking the place out. We were just walking past the Mine Shaft Tavern when we suddenly looked over and felt the smiles wipe off our faces. The front door was opening ever so slowly. It kept opening until we saw it could open no further, and it began to swing shut just as slowly. My fiancée and I just stood, gawking, until, just before it closed, it slammed the rest of the way shut. That bang was like a gunshot. We started running. It's one thing to experience something at night and then rationalize some explanation in the clear light of day. But to see that in the middle of the afternoon on a sunny day was all just too much.

Chad Brummet, Tommy Garcia and Jordan Jonas investigated the site in 2020 and spoke with the owner, Melinda Bonewell, and another bartender, Tina Walker-Highers.

When Melinda first acquired the Mine Chef Tavern, renowned as one of Madrid's most haunted places, we decided to try to cleanse it. I painted it, saged the area and recruited a Native American friend to come in with drums and sage smoke to ward off unwanted spirits. Although this seemed to rid us of all apparitions except one—the ghost of our manager's deceased husband.

Tina Walker-Highers then spoke of some of her encounters with the ghostly presence.

One night, I was locking up. Everybody was out of the tavern except for me and a server. The server was in the restroom. To your right, a mine shaft tunnel goes up to the cantina, which is our other bar. So, I'm walking out, and they're leaning. It's kind of dark, but they're leaning kind of like the Marlboro man or something. It is a cowboy, and I just see him out of my peripheral vision. That's really weird because I thought everybody had already gone. So, he's leaning against the wall with his boot up, his knee bent, and his head down. And I thought, "Wow." I started to say something to him, and I turned around, and nobody was there.

No one's gotten hurt. It doesn't seem like it's with real malice or anything, but they're very much tricksters. Like, you sit the drink down for somebody or whatever, and it just moves on its own. Now, you talk about a reaction that'll freak them out [referring to customers]. *They'll look—it's like, "Don't look at me. I didn't do it." A lot of people can't handle it. They got to go. But they're so intrigued, they always come back.*

Table 13 has a lot of stories to tell, depending on who you ask. It's been used by celebrities in the past, and it's even got a nickname: Dead Man's Corner. Rumor has it that an employee once fell asleep and passed away right there.

Customers see figures appear out of nowhere, which proves their suspicions weren't just imagined. For example, someone recently walked into the ladies' room and heard someone in one of the stalls—the door was shut, but they could hear someone talking. When they were done with their business, there was no one else in the room but the voice they heard when they entered. Immediately, people ask if this place is haunted. And while it may be easier to say no, the answer is very much yes.

The Engine House Theater used to be where the train engine 769, a 1904 Richmond steam engine, was serviced. Now, it serves as a theater and is the home of some astonishing stories. A young man visited and repeatedly encountered deceased miners that were assumed to be spirits. He believes their presences are still around.

Dead man's corner. *Photograph by the author.*

Tina Walker-Highers declared, "I'm just trying to close the bar. Leave me alone so that I can get out of here. Go and have fun without me. I tell you this every night: let me finish cleaning up the bar and locking it so it's secure; after that, it can be all yours."

5
GHOST OF THE RIO SALADO

Fifteen miles north of Socorro, I-25 intersects the Rio Salado, a tributary of the Rio Grande. The first rumored account of a haunting near the Rio Salado occurred back in 1940. On his way to El Paso, Texas, a truck driver stopped at Bernardo, near the Salas Trading Post, for a quick rest. When he woke up around 5:00 a.m., he continued his journey. Back in those days, before I-25 was built, Highway 85 crossed the old Rio Puerco bridge. It proceeded south, winding its way through the sandy hills behind today's rest area on the interstate along the banks of the Rio Salado.

As the truck approached the Rio Salado, the driver spotted a young woman walking beside it. He pumped the brakes and called out to her, asking if she needed any assistance. At first, she cried out, "It wasn't me! Take me home! I want to go back!" And then she faded away into the darkness.

The shaken truck driver sped away and eventually stopped for breakfast at the Coronado Café in Socorro, where he shared his story with anyone who was willing to listen. One of those listeners happened to be a sixteen-year-old dishwasher, who is now eighty-eight years old and still living in Socorro. He vividly remembers the frightened man and his account.

Over the years, people have repeatedly witnessed a woman walking along the highway near the Rio Salado or meandering through the riverbed with no shoes, as if she is looking for something. Individuals living in Alamillo have also heard a young woman's cries at night. Yet nobody can ever detect where they were coming from. The ghost is said to wander these parts as if searching for something or someone. Some say it's the ghost of nineteen-

The Rio Salado from the I-25 bridge. *Photograph by the author.*

year-old Rose Garcia, who was murdered, mutilated and buried in the sandy arroyo of the Rio Salado.

It is a bizarre tale that became a big story in the newspapers—a beautiful young woman killed by an older prominent Socorro businessman named Wilbur B. Cassady. The story unfolds on the pages of the *Albuquerque Journal* from November 24, 1937, in an article titled "Blood Rite Revealed in Love Letters to Slain Socorro Girl."

> *Love letters written to 19-year-old Rose Garcia are expected to play an important part in the trial of Wilbur B. Cassady, charged with first-degree murder in her slaying, it was said here Tuesday by Police Chief Pat O'Grady.*
>
> *Two letters, written on Cassady's letterheads, together with an attempt at verse-writing, were to be turned over to Valencia County officials Tuesday night. They were obtained from Teleforo Armijo, 319½ South First Street, in whose possession they have been since Sunday. Rose Garcia, Armijo said, gave them to him "to keep for her."*
>
> *The first letter, presumably written November 16, and mailed to "Mrs. Rose Montgomery" at Polvadera, referred to the home life of the writer and presumably the writer's young daughter, "Won't Be Lonesome."*
>
> *"Betty is a real pal," it read, and narrated how "Betty" had gone to a motion picture show with "her mother and Jimmy."*
>
> *On her return from the show, the letter said, "She got into bed with me and said, 'Daddy, you won't be lonesome for Rosie now that I'm here,'"*

"Really, I don't know what I'm doing part of the time," it said. "I'm going around in circles thinking of you. Please don't cheat on me. You gave me something to live for. You took my heart and left me to die by inches.

"With more love than you ever had and more kisses than you ever had, Webby."

That the writer saw the girl soon after writing the letter was evidenced in a second letter in which the writer said he "didn't sleep a wink" and asked why the girl had acted "yesterday, so cold and indifferent."

"Blood in my coffee."

"Don't you remember," it read, "the time you said you put some blood in my coffee. That made me a part of you, and only God can separate us, and I have a hunch that he will take us together."

"I was going to buy you a radio," it read and added that the writer had not bought it because she had been so "cold and indifferent" at their previous meeting. The writer suggested that he should send her bus fare so she might come to Socorro to "straighten things," and if they were not satisfactory, he would give her money to go to Silverton.

"Don't disappoint me," it read. "It may be the last chance for both of us if you do."

"With all my love, Webby."

The letters came into the possession of Arno, according to his signed statement to the police here, after he had met the girl for the first time on November 17. Armijo said he met the girl in the lobby of a hotel and that he took her to dinner several times.

She told Armijo, according to his statement, that Cassady wanted her to marry him when he had divorced his wife. Armijo also said that the girl said she was married but not residing with her husband. She also said she didn't want to marry Cassady because he had grown children.

Last Sunday, Armijo said he was walking with the girl and had gone to the Greyhound Bus station, where she got a ticket for Polvadero. While waiting for the bus they started walking around town and she suddenly saw a truck which she said belonged to Cassady.

Armijo and the girl separated, and Armijo went into a hotel lobby while the girl went to the truck. Armijo later came to the truck and asked the man if he were Cassady, he said. The man admitted his identity, shook hands with Armijo as the girl got into the truck. They drove away, Armijo told the police, and that was the last he saw of either Cassady or the girl.

Armijo was not held by the police.

The details of the murder were provided in another article in the same paper after Cassady attempted to hang himself in a cell at the county jail.

Assistant District Attorney F.M. Sedillo reported Tuesday night that W.B. Cassady attempted to hang himself in a cell at the County Jail, where he is held on charges of first-degree murder for the fatal shooting and mutilation of raven-haired Rose Garcia.

Fellow prisoners gave the alarm, Sedillo reported, and Cassady, 43-year-old businessman and father of five, was taken down but remained unconscious for several minutes.

Sedillo said Cassady had removed a small chain from his bunk, attached it to the top of the cell and around his neck, and jumped off the bunk in an effort to carry out what he repeatedly had told officers was his intention when he slew the 19-year-old housemaid with whom he was in love. The girl's body was found in a shallow sand grave early Tuesday.

Turned over to authorities in Socorro late Sunday by a physician to whom Cassady had come for "something to end it all," he broke under hours of grilling by Socorro County officers and state police and directed them to the crude grave, where the girl was buried along the Rio Salado, in the backcountry, 17 miles north of Socorro.

"I was crazy about her—we were crazy about each other," he sobbed to Sheriff Frank Knoblock of Socorro County, and Sheriff Henry Jaramillo of Valencia County, after signing a full purported confession to the slaying.

Assistant District Attorney F.M. Sedillo said Cassady, under further questioning by him and Jaramillo, corroborated his alleged confession and said his only desire "was the electric chair as quick as possible."

"He is eager to get it over," said Sedillo.

As a grim crowd of ranchers and residents of Socorro congregated in the morning in front of the courthouse, Cassady was spirited from here to Los Lunas, neighboring county seat, where he waived preliminary hearing and pleaded innocent to the murder charge, signed by State Police Sergeant Joe T. Roach.

After lengthy further questioning in the Valencia County Jail here, District Attorney John Baron Burg, who led the party that found the body, ordered Cassady held here pending order from the court.

The girl's body, with a bullet through her breast and horribly mutilated, was exhumed about 1 a.m. under the lights of blazing bonfires and the glare of headlights from the automobiles of the searching posse, Sergeant Roach said a penknife had been used on the girl's body.

Sheriff Frank Knoblock quoted Cassady's alleged confession as stating he shot the girl when she took Cassady's pistol, pointed it dramatically at her breast, and "begged" him to shoot.

He intended to kill himself, Cassady's confession added, but he said he lost his "nerve" and didn't remember anything further until he found himself driving home with the body of the girl in the back of his light truck.

"The sheriff and the state policemen," he said in a jail cell interview, "told me I cut her up, but I don't remember anything about that."

Sheriff Knoblock said the girl went to Albuquerque last week, and Cassady, frantic she would leave him, followed her there Sunday. He argued her into returning home with him, and the shooting allegedly occurred as they talked in the car on a side road near Isleta Pueblo, about 12 miles south of Albuquerque.

Among the girl's possessions were found passionate love letters signed "Webby," one of which said: "Only God can separate us, and I have a hunch he will soon take us both together."

An unsigned poem was also among the effects, reading:

"All night, I keep listening for the patter of her feet,
Coming down the lonely hallway.
Wait, my heart almost skipped a beat,
For, at last, though I heard them,
Pitter-patter as before.
But alas, I'm disappointed,
Won't they ever come no more?"

Cassady, a small, thin-faced, blue-eyed man, trembled visibly as he sat in the Valencia County Jail and talked with Sheriffs Knoblock and Jaramillo and an Associated Press staff reporter.

He told how Rose had left him a week ago and came to Albuquerque. On Thursday of last week, he said, he and Guadalupe Garcia, the girl's father, had gone to Albuquerque in an attempt to argue her into returning to Socorro. She had angrily refused, he said.

On Sunday, he said, he came back again and found her "ready to come back." They had dinner, saw a movie, and started on the drive home.

At Isleta, he said, the girl asked him to pull off on the side of the road for a talk. There, he declared, she "begged" him to shoot her and pointed the pistol at her breast, asking him to pull the trigger.

At this point in his interview, however, his account of what happened next differed from that which he made in his signed confession.

Cassady said he did not shoot her but that she killed herself in a struggle for possession of the gun after she had threatened to kill herself and Cassady, too. From that point, the prisoner remembered nothing until he "came to" passing through Belen.

At Socorro, he said, he drove to Rose's home intending to tell her father Rose was killed in a struggle for the gun. No one answered his knock, he continued, and he drove out into the country, where he dug a grave and buried the girl.

"I have a wife and five children," he said. "My wife just got back from the state hospital in Las Vegas. I was afraid the same thing was going to happen to me. Both my wife and myself have not been in good health, and the girl was a little batty, too."

After returning home from burying the body, Cassady then said he went to a doctor and asked him for "something to put me out of the way." "If the doctor had been a man, he would have given me something and saved the state a lot of money and my family from disgrace."

The *Reno Gazette-Journal* recorded the outcome of the murder on August 15, 1938.

Adjudged guilty of involuntary manslaughter in the slaying Rose Garcia, a pretty nineteen-year-old Socorro girl who had been his housekeeper, W.B. Cassady, Socorro laundry operator, faced today a nine- to ten-year term in the state prison. A district court jury reached its verdict at 8:50 a.m. Sunday, after nearly nine hours of deliberation. Denying the defense motion for a new trial, Judge George W. Hay immediately passed sentence on the middle-aged Cassady, thrice married and father of five children. Ten years is the maximum penalty for a manslaughter conviction in New Mexico. The Garcia girl was shot, her body mutilated, last November 21. Officers led by Cassady found her body buried under a little sand dune several miles north of Socorro. The state charged Cassady with her murder. The trial's testimony brought from Cassady the admission he and the girl had been living as man and wife for several months while his wife was in the state hospital. He testified the girl was fatally shot as she was attempting suicide and as he was trying to take the gun away from her.

I find it odd that Cassady was charged with only manslaughter, especially considering the gory details of the murder. The final twist came on November 30, 1939, in the pages of the *Albuquerque Journal*.

> *W.B. Cassady, Socorro laundryman convicted of killing his housemaid sweetheart, recently underwent several months' treatment at the state mental hospital, Las Vegas, it was revealed Wednesday. Warden John B. McManus said the man responded satisfactorily and had been returned to the state prison, where he was sent after a jury found him guilty of shooting Rosa Garcia to death in a fit of jealousy. "I'm afraid I'm a little crazy," Cassady told officers and newsmen before his trial.*

Stories of a ghost near the Rio Salado persisted for many years before waning when Interstate 25 was constructed in 1964, replacing U.S. Highway 85. My first experience with the ghost story came in 2005 at a social gathering in Socorro. I was planning a Halloween ghost tour and wanted to include any local ghost stories I could find. As people began to drink, I saw that one of my former wife's friends had a husband who worked as a state trooper. Police officers often witness bizarre occurrences but don't usually talk about them with citizens. Once he had consumed some drinks, I approached him. I explained that I was looking for local paranormal-related tales and asked if he had been privy to anything peculiar nearby.

Behind this gate are the remnants of Highway 85 and the bridge that once crossed the Rio Salado. *Photograph by the author.*

He recounted his experience working the Acacia weigh station, one mile south of the rest area at mile marker 166. He had just finished up for the day and was about to leave when he heard a woman shouting for help in the distance. This voice seemed to be coming from the northwest, so he hopped over the wire fence and set off in that direction. After trekking fifty feet, he came upon an old road (U.S. Highway 85) that ran north. The woman's cries were getting louder, so he followed the roadway for roughly three-fourths of a mile until he finally noticed a big sandy arroyo (the Rio Salado). Standing in the arroyo and waving her arms, there was a figure silhouetted against the horizon—a woman. When he shined his flashlight toward her, she immediately vanished.

The officer recalled that he sprinted toward where he'd last seen her, but she was nowhere to be found. He fervently searched the Rio Salado and suddenly felt a shiver down his spine. The hair on the back of his neck stood up, and he spun around, hoping to find anyone or anything that could explain this sensation. To his dismay, he couldn't spot a soul. Embarrassed from realizing that nerves might have gotten the better of him, the officer abandoned the search and returned to his patrol car.

"I've been back to the weigh station since then," he explained. "But I have never encountered something like that again. It's on the wildlife refuge, so it is closed to the public and out in the middle of nowhere. If it was a woman, I have no idea how she would have evaded me."

The second ghost story I heard came from a couple who attended an event I hosted at the Garcia Opera House in Socorro. I was discussing the Battle of Valverde, and after my presentation, they approached me to say they had seen La Llorona in the arroyo near the rest stop north of San Acacia. The couple was driving back to Socorro after attending a late-night wedding in Albuquerque. They were exhausted, and the darkness outside made them feel uneasy. As they passed the rest stop north of San Acacia, they saw a figure walking in the distance along the arroyo. The woman was dressed in a long gray dress and looked distraught. She was waving her arms around like she was arguing with someone. The couple slowed their car to get a better look when the husband suggested it might be La Llorona. They were afraid and didn't know what to do, so they drove away as fast as possible. After telling them the story I had heard from the state trooper, we all wondered if they had seen the same supernatural figure.

Does the spirit of the Rio Salado belong to Rose Garcia? Or is it La Llorona? Perhaps it is someone else, some unknown woman who lost her life in the arroyo and now seeks solace. We may never know.

6

THE GHOSTS OF SOCORRO

When the Val Verde Hotel opened in 1919, the *Albuquerque Morning Journal* covered the event and noted, "From the standpoint of beauty and convenience, she stands without a peer."

Designed by architect Henry Trost and built just after World War I, the Val Verde Hotel was a true gem in Socorro. The building was constructed with elegance and style, and it quickly became the most sought-after place to stay in the city.

Above the hotel's fireplace hangs an artistic desert landscape painted by Peter J. Savage and signed by him. Savage moved to Socorro, New Mexico, for health reasons in 1923 and painted compulsively in exchange for his living arrangements. The upper walls of the hotel's dining room proudly display Savage's unique mountain scenes ranging from El Paso to Albuquerque. Mrs. Apodaca completed any gaps in the mural with her own desert images. The dinner table and bathrooms were decorated in a deep jade color. The building was highlighted with original brass light fixtures, old-fashioned brass radiators, an oak phone booth, pedestal sinks and a walk-in wooden refrigerator with meat hanging on hooks, which was later used to store wines.

The Val Verde resembled two other famous hotels, Albuquerque's Alvarado and Las Vegas's Castaneda, but it had no connection to Santa Fe Railway or Fred Harvey. Though it was located just a few blocks from the railroad tracks, passengers still had to trudge along a dusty path or take Cook's livery to reach the hotel. The dining room menu featured fresh seafood delights, out-of-season strawberries and local ingredients like wild asparagus.

The Val Verde Hotel opened in 1919. The *Albuquerque Morning Journal* claimed that "from the standpoint of beauty and convenience, she stands without a peer." *Library of Congress.*

Built for $65,000 by the Socorro Holding Co., the hotel was first managed by C.L. Snyder, Mrs. Paxton's brother-in-law, but the Paxtons were called from Kansas City to help out when he died in 1922 and returned when Mrs. Snyder became ill in 1929.

After the hotel had been owned by the Paxtons for only a few days, it was transformed into a Red Cross hub to aid those affected by the flood that destroyed San Marcial, a nearby railroad town. It later became an oft-visited spot for governors of New Mexico and hosted famous visitors like Will Rogers and Conrad Hilton.

It was strange to learn that the Val Verde Hotel might be haunted, as I first heard of it from my friend Buck, who lived there in 2001. Back then, the rooms on the second floor were rented out as apartments, with two old rooms composing each apartment. Except for a few "grander" suites, the rooms share two common bathrooms on the second floor. Each room is equipped with its own shower. Inside the building, one staircase leads to the

The hotel in the 1930s. *National Park Service.*

upper floor. This door is locked, so the second floor can be accessed by two fire escapes located at the rear of the building. These are the stairs that the tenants used for access to their apartments.

One day, Buck invited me to his place to look into the peculiar happenings in his room. When I arrived, he pointed out that all the dresser drawers and cabinet doors were wide open. He told me this always occurred; each time he returned, they would be opened again, despite being shut already. Being ghost hunters, we started asking around.

We were told about the rumors of a catastrophic boiler explosion that took place there in the 1920s, leading to the deaths of five men. Supposedly, this is one of the reasons the old building is haunted. The evidence seems to support this tragic incident, as the boiler room reveals several scorched timbers and old repair work to the floor joists and supports. However, my search for any newspaper articles on the accident was fruitless. However, an incident in 1929 may explain some of the damage. The event was chronicled in the *Albuquerque Journal* on November 25, 1929.

> *Fire suspected to be of incendiary origin broke out in the Socorro Steam Laundry, adjacent to the Val Verde Hotel, in Socorro early Sunday morning and after resisting the efforts of the local department for several hours left it a mass of smoldering ruins with loss estimated at $15,000.*

The Val Verde Hotel as it appeared in the early 1970s. *National Park Service.*

The two buildings occupied by the laundry, facing Manzanares Avenue, were totally destroyed with all equipment, some of which had only recently been installed. One of the buildings was of adobe construction, and the other brick and crumbling walls endangered the volunteers under Fire Chief F.D. Miller, keeping them from entering the blazing structures. Frank Chambon and Percy Sickles, directing a stream through a window of the adobe building, narrowly escaped injury when the wall collapsed. Two high-pressure streams from the pumper engine were kept on the blaze for three hours before it subsided.

The flames were first noticed at 3:30 a.m. Sunday by Lorenzo Baca, night clerk of the Val Verde Hotel, which was separated from the laundry by a small thoroughfare. By that time, the fire had gained full headway, and the volunteers devoted their efforts to keep It from spreading.

The incendiarism theory was established by Chief Miller after an investigation. The laundry had been broken into the night before, he informed the Journal, *"but the prowlers were frightened off by the arrival of a driver. They evidently came back Saturday night and started the fire accidentally or maliciously."*

The loss was reported at $15,000 by S.Y. Jackson, manager of the Excelsior Laundry in Albuquerque, who was called to Socorro by W.B. Cassady, proprietor of the laundry burnt out. Arrangements were *made for the temporary handling of the Socorro business through the Albuquerque laundry.*

The loss was 50 percent covered, according to Mr. Jackson.

So, while there may not be any deaths connected to the boiler explosion, there are many people who have died by suicide in the building. As we investigated further, I discovered that one such incident had occurred in the room that Buck was renting. It was recorded in the *Albuquerque Tribune* on August 29, 1938.

James O. Guleke, 47, attorney of Amarillo, Texas, was found shot to death in a Val Verde Hotel room here early today. A coroner's jury held he had committed suicide. The body was found at 7 a.m. by friends who sought to awaken him and, receiving no response, broke down the room door, locked from the inside. A revolver bullet had pierced his forehead.

Dr. V.E. Franklin said Mr. Guleke had been dead since about 6 a.m. Sheriff Frank Knoblock said there was no indication of the motive but added he had learned Mr. Guleke left Amarillo recently to recuperate from a nervous breakdown. He registered at the hotel here last night. Mr. Guleke was accompanied by Mr. and Mrs. Loy Smith of Amarillo. They remained in seclusion at the hotel.

Perhaps it is nothing more than coincidence, but it was enough for Buck to move into another room.

Back in 2001, ghost hunting was not a well-known activity. When the restaurant employees heard that we were looking into the strange events that were happening at the hotel, they were happy to talk to us about what they had experienced themselves.

Apparently, the bartenders hear a thumping sound under the floor of the bar. They believe it is the workers who died in the fire banging on the ceiling with shovels or other tools.

Cinde Trott, a waitress of ten years in Val Verde, mentioned that another waitress, who no longer works there, heard an eerie voice call out, "How are you, my darling?"

"She started crying," Trott said.

Trott recalled that once, she was in the waitress station when a pitcher, perched on top of the ice freezer, suddenly flew off and smashed a glass several feet away near the sink. However, she is not the only employee who has had strange experiences while working at the Val Verde.

The aging sign of the hotel and its former restaurant. *Library of Congress.*

Another suicide occurred while Buck was living in the hotel. The white powder on the floor is a deodorant that was placed where the body had decomposed. *Photograph by the author.*

"A few times I've been down in the basement, I've had the impression somebody's behind me," said waiter Chris Parra. "Some customers would say there was someone in the restroom when no one was around, or they could hear odd noises. Others just felt like someone was watching them."

Val Verde employee Fran Calderon said a woman in a blue dress and a man wearing a white shirt had made an appearance in the bar. Calderon also said a Val Verde manager once saw a "weird light" in one of the rooms at the steakhouse and felt a bizarre static electricity.

"It made the hair on the back of their neck stand up, and it made their skin kind of red," she said. "It's a weird feeling you get. It's not scary, but you can actually feel their [the ghosts'] presence. It doesn't make you uncomfortable."

Another strange event occurred late at night after the restaurant had closed. As they do at all restaurants, the staff had many hours of work ahead to clean the kitchen, scrub the cookware and set up for the next day's service. It was a typical evening, but this one would turn out to be different. That evening, a truck delivered boxes filled with food and supplies to the back door of the kitchen. After the cleanup was done, these boxes needed to be taken to the basement for storage. The chef and his assistant made multiple trips, carrying armfuls of boxes down to the basement before returning upstairs for more.

Paranormal investigators search the hotel. *Photograph by the author.*

The chef was on his last round in the kitchen when he suddenly realized he couldn't remember where his assistant was. As he prepared to leave, he looked down the small staircase to see if the prep cook was there. Instead of seeing his companion, however, an "older man in a suit and half-shaven" stared up at him from the bottom step. Thinking he must be getting pranked, he shouted, "What are you doing here?" His question was immediately answered by a voice that came from the kitchen. Apparently, his helper had not deserted him after all. Catching sight of his boss's stupefied expression, the prep cook joined him at the stairs, only to be confronted with the same elderly figure looking up at them both.

The two men locked eyes with this mysterious stranger before looking back at each other. When they looked back down the stairs, the elderly man was gone. The two horrified men fled from the kitchen without turning off the lights and tried to explain what they had experienced to their colleagues. As their coworkers stepped cautiously into the kitchen, all eyes were diverted toward the stairs that led down into a pitch-black cellar. But there was nothing to observe; somehow, the stairway's lights had been snuffed out.

The half-shaven man seemed to appear sporadically over the years. A worker or two would see the old man with his face half-shaven, often in the basement or dining room or walking into the men's restroom after hours. The restaurant owners never saw him, but they could tell when their employees had a run-in; they'd be left shaken. Many believe the man might be the original proprietor of the Val Verde Hotel or someone who died by suicide in the building long ago.

Socorro has many eerie tales that have been handed down through its local history, which Dorothy J. Baylor collected in 1947. The following are ten of my favorite stories she recorded.

INDIAN GHOST AS FLOWER

TOLD IN SPANISH TO ELOISA MARTINEZ BY HER FATHER

There were three brothers who were sent by their father to camp. While there, the two elder brothers were so envious of their younger brother that they killed him and buried him up there. No one knew about him or heard of him again.

One day, a Native who was roaming around was attracted by a flower, a beautiful flower. This flower happened to be on top of the grave of the buried man. This Native cut the flower and smelled it. While he was smelling it, the flower talked to him.

It said that he was killed at camp and that he should talk to him with sorrow. The Native took this flower to the chief, and the flower said the same thing to him. The chief had all the town people over, and he passed this flower to all of them. When the flower was passed to the two brothers, it said something different. It said that they should talk to it with sorrow, for they had killed him. This is how it was revealed that the two brothers had killed the younger brother.

GHOST TAKES MAN

CONTRIBUTED BY AGUINALDO BACA

This story was told by an old man who died several years ago. He used to say that when he was in his fifties, he used to ride a horse almost every day. There were always two persons with him, his two best friends.

He claimed that almost every day, for two weeks, while he and his companions were passing through a wooded path, they would see a ghost in front of them. They could not make out what it was, for it was covered from head to foot. He ran about fifty feet in front of the horses, and the riders could never catch up with him. Later, one of the three men died.

The other two claimed that the ghost was his guardian angel and had been trying to take him. He had never had the chance until the night the man was alone.

PRIEST RETURNS BECAUSE OF UNFINISHED MASSES

TOLD BY SISTER MELITINA TO JOE ARMIJO

A priest made a promise that if his wish came true, he would go to the church at midnight and say some prayers. It so happened that he got his wish. That night, he went to the church and started saying his prayers. Halfway through his prayers, he looked up toward the altar, and to his surprise, there stood a man dressed in priest's garments. He knew he had never seen this priest in his parish before, and he didn't recall anyone mentioning anything about a new priest coming to the parish. Then he noticed something peculiar about this new person standing before him; he could see through him.

This made him so scared that he froze. The intruder moved closer to the frightened priest and said in a faraway tone, "Do not be afraid; what you are thinking is true. I am a ghost. I would like to ask of you a favor, but first let me tell you the reason for my being here. Some years ago, I made a promise to give twenty masses; and, in case I never lived to complete my promise, I vowed to come back and finish. I've been coming every night for a number of years, but I haven't found anyone to serve mass for me yet. Tonight, you happened to come, and now I want to ask you to do this favor for me."

The priest served the mass. The next morning, priests asked him about it, and he told them about the night before.

Ghostly Return Because of an Unfulfilled Promise

TOLD IN SPANISH BY LUCIA ORTIZ TO TOM CRESPIN

When my aunt was about ten years old, her aunt promised to give my aunt a fryer and a pullet whenever her baby chicks grew up. My aunt was always helping her aunt with the chickens.

One night, my aunt and a Mrs. Chavez went to their friend's house, which was about a quarter of a mile away. My aunt was never afraid in her life, but this particular night, she was very much afraid on the way up and back. When my aunt and Mrs. Chavez were coming back home, my aunt saw a light in the house. My aunt went in the house and saw her aunt sitting next to the fireplace. There wasn't any light in the room.

My aunt talked to her aunt, who was sitting next to the fireplace, but she didn't respond. They locked the door and went to the kitchen. When Mr. Chavez came from town, he told them that my aunt's aunt had died that night. They went over to see if there was anybody in the room my aunt and Mrs. Chavez had locked. There wasn't anybody there. They went in the kitchen, where they sat eating some candy. As my aunt turned around, she saw her aunt. Then my aunt remembered the fryer and pullet her aunt had promised her and told her that she need not bother to give her the fryer and the pullet. From then on, she never bothered my aunt.

Ghost Attends Dance

TOLD TO LUCY PADILLA BY HER SISTER JACKIE PADILLA

A girl in a beautiful white gown attended a dance two years ago. This girl was different from any other girl at the dance. She was pale and had a frozen look. A service boy spotted her and later asked her to dance. They danced together all night long. The girl didn't talk unless the boy asked questions.

After the dance was over, the boy took her home. Because she was so cold and stiff, he lent her his jacket. When they neared a graveyard, the girl said, "This is where I live. If you want your jacket, go over to my house for it. You know where I live." She then disappeared. The boy stood motionless and knew that she must have been a ghost. He returned to camp very frightened.

The next morning, he decided to go get his jacket. He asked the girl's mother for his jacket. The lady was puzzled and thought maybe he was crazy. The boy said, "Your daughter borrowed my jacket last night."

The woman said, "I have no daughter. I did have one, but she's been dead for five years."

The boy was very frightened because the mother told him to go to the grave—maybe he would find his jacket there. He went, and there it was, spread over the grave. The service boy couldn't believe this. He told his buddies about it, but no one believed him.

This news spread around soon. To confirm the boy's story, they dug up the girl's remains, and she appeared just as she had at the dance—and the way they had buried her. Even her orchid was fresh. This story is true, and many people who attended the dance saw her. Afterward, this boy didn't attend any dances for fear that this girl might reappear.

Ghost Haunts Murderess

CONTRIBUTED BY MARION ESQUIVEL

Not long ago, a lady murdered an old man. She is now in prison. Her daughter claims that she cannot eat nor sleep, and every time she tries to eat or sleep, she can see the man everywhere she goes. He follows her.

GHOST SOUNDS

In an old, haunted house on Highway 85 at about 12:00 a.m., you can hear the rattle of bottles and then the wails of a lonely woman. The explanation to this is that many years ago, a couple lived in this house very happily until one night, at about 12:00 a.m., the man went down to the wine cellar to set a mouse trap. While he was going down the stairs, he tripped and fell and hit the table leg with his head and knocked some bottles to the floor. Then his wife, after hearing the noise, ran downstairs to find her husband dead. That is why you can hear these sounds in the still of the night.

A GHOST ANSWERS

TOLD TO DORRIS OLSEN BY MRS. W.L. JONES

One dark night, as a drunk man was on his way home, he fell into a sunken grave beside the road. He was so drunk that he just stayed there. A few minutes later, two men came riding by, and they stopped. One man pointed to the sunken grave and said, "The meanest man in the world is lying there."

The drunk man in the grave raised himself up and said, "You're a big liar. I am not the meanest man in the world." The other two men started to run, and then when they came to their senses, they found that they were five miles away from home.

DEATH ALLEY

TOLD BY MRS. MIRES TO BURDIE CALDWELL AND BARBARA STIRLING

Death Alley is now called Garfield Avenue. It got its name from the many illegal hangings that occurred there. At one of these particular hangings, the victim said, "I place my curse on Socorro for this illegal hanging, and as long as anyone of you are alive, this town will never prosper."

7

BELEN HARVEY HOUSE

T he people of Belen, New Mexico, received a wonderful surprise in December 1910 from the Atchison, Topeka and Santa Fe Railway. After dealing with multiple financial issues and engineering problems, the railroad finished its extension through Abo Canyon and arrived in Belen in 1909. This was labeled the Belen Cut-Off, which was now a central hub for all trains moving north–south and east–west. Shortly afterward, it was declared the "Hub City" of New Mexico. It gained another benefit: a Harvey House train restaurant just north of its depot on South First Street. The Harvey House fed hungry passengers of the Santa Fe lines as well as their employees, who needed delicious food and quick service no matter what time it was.

The Harvey House in Belen remained functional for the following twenty-nine years, through World War I, the Roaring Twenties and almost the entirety of the Great Depression. Hundreds of staff members were employed over its lifespan, including Fred Harvey's most famous employees, known as the Harvey Girls. The hard work of the Harvey Girls was handsomely rewarded. Each month, they earned a salary and were also given free accommodations and food, plus they sometimes received very generous gratuities.

During their free time, the Harvey Girls often went to the post office, shopped at Becker-Dalies, watched movies in town and played croquet on the south lawn of the Harvey House. They also built snowmen in winter and sunbathed on top of the house in the summer. Whenever new Harvey Girls were hired, it was quite an event for the locals—many young men

The Belen Harvey House in the late 1950s. *Library of Congress*

found excuses to visit the house just to see them. Despite rules against dating colleagues, some Harvey Girls met their husbands at work.

The Belen Harvey House flourished until the start of the Great Depression. Automobiles and buses became increasingly pervasive, as did trains with more economical fares and improved dining cars, making it difficult for the old Harvey Houses to compete. Passengers who ate all three meals in a dining car could pay only ninety cents daily. Consequently, forty-nine Harvey Houses closed in the 1930s, including those in Vaughn, Lamy and Rincon. Finally, Belen's facility met its demise in 1939.

Though many mourned the loss of the Harvey House, it was far from finished. Within a short time, it would experience three significant transformations in its long life. First, the Santa Fe Railway breathed new life into the building by repurposing it into a Reading Room, with an official opening slated for May 1940. Belen's Reading Room wasn't especially grand or large, but it was on par with those in the other railroad towns in New Mexico. By 1913, the library boasted a selection that could "hold its own" against those in larger cities.

The Reading Room in Belen had been a major success, but it all changed during the 1930s. The railroad couldn't afford to keep it running anymore, and by 1938, it stopped offering any entertainment. It officially closed one year later, in 1939, at the same time the town's beloved Harvey House closed.

Business was booming in Belen leading up to World War II. This prompted the need for a new Reading Room that was larger than its predecessor. In May 1941, the old Harvey House became that space, and for the first time ever, it was able to become the "hotel" that had been written into its original building contract of 1910.

The demand for sleeping quarters was so overwhelming that 16,327 men stayed in the Reading Room in 1956 alone. To fit more people, two bathrooms and a sunroom were added to the south end of what used to be the lunchroom. Even with this increase in space, employees had to wait for hours before getting a bed. Some never got beds and resorted to temporarily sleeping in chairs or on oversized tables. A sign cautioned them to keep their shoes off the furniture but said they were welcome to put their feet up. One-time reservations were impossible to get; guests had to check out and then back in on the same day, hoping they wouldn't have to wait too long for their next stay.

By the 1970s, it was apparent to everyone that the Belen Reading Room needed some serious updating and repairs if it was going to remain open. The Santa Fe Railway had fewer staff members, largely due to newer technologies and diesel engines. Unfortunately, they weren't willing to pay for a costly remodel for a place that no longer needs as much use. So, on September 2, 1980, Belen's Reading Room closed its doors for good.

That fall, the entrance to the Reading Room was blocked off. Most residents of Belen figured it wouldn't be long until the Santa Fe Railroad tore the building down, just like it had with so many of its faded Harvey Houses. However, the wreckage of the Alvarado in Albuquerque sparked shock and dread among Belen's civic leaders, who worked to ensure their own Harvey House would never suffer the same demise. The Save the Harvey House Committee was formed to preserve the building for its historic importance and its potential to bring tourism and stimulate local economic growth. Gentry and his associates reasoned that it was important to save the famous old restaurant not only for its historical significance but also to draw people in from around the area.

The *Valencia County News-Bulletin* also played a huge role in preserving the building. Gary Herron wrote multiple articles about the historical significance of the building and details of those trying to stop the demolition plans. The newspaper was so dedicated that it even received the New Mexico Press Association's Public Service Award for its hard work in thwarting the

Eventually, the old Harvey House became a community center. *Photograph by the author.*

One of the upstairs rooms that housed the Harvey girls. *Photograph by the author.*

building's destruction. Thankfully, these valiant efforts did not go to waste. On February 3, 1983, the Santa Fe Railway reversed its decision and handed over the Harvey House building to Belen City. That summer, twenty inmates from Los Lunas Penal Farm were sent to help sanitize and paint the walls.

When the city realized there was a need for a community center, the Harvey House entered its third phase. The lunchroom area was cleared out and open for public events, such as aerobic classes, wedding receptions and high school graduation parties. Additionally, upstairs offices were available for nonprofit organizations like the New Mexico Country Music Association.

However, running the facility as a community center posed a challenge to maintaining one of the oldest buildings in Belen. The chamber of commerce and other organizations that occupied it cycled in and out frequently. And the "big room" went through considerable wear and tear due to all the happenings that took place there, especially when alcohol was consumed. Eventually, in the late 1990s, city officials determined that the Harvey House was no longer viable as a community center and decided to discontinue its operations.

The old Harvey House building is now in its fourth stage, serving as a museum for the Belen Model Railroad Club and the Valencia County Historical Society.

The Harvey House Museum is a constantly evolving space. It hosts special exhibits, even some from the Smithsonian Institution in Washington, D.C., in the former lunchroom. Visitors can enjoy two semiannual railroad shows, quilt shows and art displays hosted by the Belen Art League. The building is rumored to be haunted. One of the first mentions of paranormal activity came on September 27, 2016, from KRQE news.

Some say it's haunted; ghost hunters couldn't resist making the Harvey House Museum in Belen part of the world's largest ghost hunt. This weekend, dozens of people will go looking for paranormal activity inside of it. It's part of National Ghost Hunting Day.

The Harvey House even had to be recognized by paranormal professionals as a verified haunted location. The now-museum sits along the train tracks in Belen, but from 1910 to the late 1930s, it served as a restaurant for passengers. Frances Zeller is the director of the museum. She said they couldn't have picked a better spot to ghost hunt.

"I notice that sometimes lights are on when I thought I turned them off, or lights are off when I thought I turned on," she said. "Sometimes, I scratch myself on the head and wonder, 'What's going on here?'"

Shonda Murillo and her team, Lunatic Devine Ghost Hunting, will break up into three groups on October 1. They will divide the three floors of the museum.

"This will be the first time we're going down to the basement," she said. "We only know of what other people have caught down there."

But when Murillo first presented the idea of holding the event, they did an initial walk-through with all of their special ghost hunting equipment.

"We did catch an apparition, and we had to make sure it wasn't any of our team members," Murillo said. "She was walking into one of the rooms; we're pretty sure it was a Harvey girl because she was dressed up in the Harvey girl outfit."

After studying the newspaper archives, I found no reports of death or traumatic events occurring in the building. All the events celebrated there were positive ones, such as wedding receptions and parties. Additionally, there have been no ghost stories associated with the building before the twenty-first century. Even so, this does not rule out the possibility of a spirit living there. The ghost of Abraham Lincoln has been seen in the White House by Winston Churchill and Eleanor Roosevelt, yet the former president did not die there. So, perhaps these merry events is what has attracted a spirit to the Harvey House Museum.

Another newspaper article that covered the hauntings at the old building was published by the *Valencia County News-Bulletin* on Halloween 2019.

Call them ghosts or spirits, but they have made their mark in some of Valencia County's most notable establishments. Many say they've seen or heard them, but are they really there?

Ronnie Torres had a few paranormal encounters during his time at the Belen Harvey House Museum.

About seven years ago, during the Festival of Trees event, Torres would go to the museum at night by himself. He would make the trek to the second floor to decorate the trees.

"One night, I was up there, and I could hear some conversation and laughing downstairs. I thought somebody must have come in," Torres said.

He thought it was strange because of the late hour, but he went back to his tasks until he heard it again.

Torres couldn't understand what was being said, only that it sounded like a couple of ladies conversing. He wanted to go downstairs and let whoever was down there know that he was upstairs so he wouldn't startle them.

"When I went downstairs, no one was there," he remembers. "The doors were locked, the lights were off, so I was the only one there."

Torres said it wasn't scary for him because he felt like there was good energy there.

"I said out loud, 'If there's anybody here, let me finish decorating the trees, and then you can put the star on top.'" Torres said with a chuckle.

In another instance, Torres was upstairs again. At the time, there were bars at the entrance of most of the rooms.

"I was standing there, looking at the shadow from the light, and the figure of someone walked across that shadow," Torres said.

No one was supposed to be in the Harvey House at that time, so he went to the next room. Again, the room was empty, the doors were locked.

"It couldn't have been a shadow from a bird or anything because we had the windows completely covered with Styrofoam," he said. "The shadow would've had to been made from someone walking through the light in the room."

Paranormal investigators have gone through the museum and confirmed the upstairs is a "hot spot" for ghost activity.

"There's been quite a few people who have experienced something in there," Torres said. "That's where the idea for the annual ghost-hunting tour came from."

Cynthia Shetter, the director of the Los Lunas Public Library, is no stranger to paranormal experiences at the library.

Shetter recalls a specific instance years ago during the summer when something unexplained occurred.

"One day, this Native American man came in and was wearing a duster [an ankle-length coat] with tall boots," Shetter recalls. "He looked like he came straight out of a history book."

Shetter started watching the man as he was sitting near the reference desk, looking through books. She said there was another man with him, but the first man stood out to her.

"I saw them walk up and go to another room," Shetter said. "When I got up to follow them, I could not find them. I came back and asked the staff where those men went, and everyone asked, 'What guys? We never saw anyone sitting right there.'"

Shetter didn't think much of it until something similar occurred later, when another employee started seeing the same man with a similar description that disappears.

"We are the only two who have seen this man," Shetter said.

Paranormal investigators have come to the Los Lunas Public Library to see if they can find evidence of spirits.

"They set up cameras, and they caught orbs during the day," Shetter said. "Then we did it at night, and they caught a bunch of orbs. They said everywhere I walked, there were several orbs following me."

Orbs are circular particles on an image that can be created from a reflection, dust, water droplets, or particles floating in the air. In paranormal investigations, ghost hunters believe orbs that remain in a series of photographs can be manifestations of ghost energy.

For Halloween one year, Shetter and the staff decided to have paranormal investigators go through the building after hours to see what they found.

"Everyone is always freaked out by the teen room," Shetter said. "They don't like to be back there by themselves; staff doesn't like to work in their alone; people hear books moving and things like that."

The investigator did a walk-through of the building and was drawn right away to the teen room. The group of people there entered the teen room and stood in a circle.

"The hair on my neck stood up, and I got goosebumps and said, 'Here they come.'"

Shetter believes everything she has encountered so far is good.

"It felt like a rush of puppies coming up to greet me. It was like whatever was there that night was happy to see me."

There used to be a large tree behind the library building. Shetter said it had indentations from where a rope was—it was a hanging tree.

The upstairs area of the building has a reputation for being haunted, and some rooms have an exceptionally high concentration of supernatural phenomena. The uniform room is said to be one of these locations. The room contains two sets of garb that are thought to be haunted. One outfit is from World War I, while the other is a nurses' uniform from World War II.

Rumor has it that the basement of the Harvey House is another paranormal hotspot. Creeping down the claustrophobic staircase, you feel chills when you reach the stone-floored basement. It's dimly lit and spooky. There are rooms full of holiday decorations and creepy mannequins that make the atmosphere even more unnerving.

But one spot stands out from the rest: the boiler room in the basement. It's like a complex combination of both old-fashioned equipment and modern technology. It was in this area that another ghostly encounter took place.

The basement is reported to be one of the most haunted areas in the building. *Photograph by the author.*

The man who witnessed it was a paranormal investigator who emailed me about his encounter.

He shivered, and his heart quickened as he descended into the dank basement alone. All he could hear was the muffled sound of his breathing until a terrible chill began to set in. He turned on his thermal imaging camera and swept it across the boiler room.

At first, nothing seemed out of place. But then, in the corner of the room, he spotted an unnatural shape. Initially, it was faint and hazy but gained definition with each passing second. His eyes widened as he realized it was a man dressed in clothing from another era. He had short, dark hair and a look of despair in his eyes. The investigator gulped as he slowly approached him, calling out. Yet the figure remained silent—until he suddenly faded away into thin air, leaving the investigator alone in the murky darkness.

"I believe that it was a railroad worker," the man said in the email. "It appeared to me that he was looking for something, although I have no idea what it is."

8
SHAFFER HOTEL

The Shaffer Hotel was built in 1923 by Clem "Pop" Shaffer, who moved to Mountainair in 1908 with his wife, Pearl, to practice his blacksmith trade. He set up his blacksmith shop with an adjacent hardware and casket-making shop on Main Street, but Pearl died of pneumonia before the end of their first year in town. Shaffer married his second wife, Lena Imboden, a native of Mountainair, in 1913. The two were fortunate enough to strike good water behind the blacksmith shop. Shaffer began selling piped water to the nearby businesses and barrels to locals at ten cents each. Unfortunately, the blacksmith shop and hardware store burned down in 1922.

Soon afterward, local residents convinced Shaffer to build a hotel on the site of his old shop, and, understandably dubious of wooden structures, he built the cast-concrete Shaffer Hotel, the concrete reinforced with iron scraps or fractions from his now-defunct blacksmith business. He continued to modify the property, adding the restaurant in 1929 with its original ceiling artwork and chandeliers and the rock-inlaid fence surrounding the property. There are reports that a Ford dealership and garage once operated behind the hotel and that the coffin workshop continued its operations.

Soon, a new restaurant opened next door to the Shaffer Hotel, its ceiling ornately adorned with intricate carvings and rich colors. Every day, Lena, Pop's second wife, would do her daily grocery shopping, providing Pop with a few extra moments of leisure. One day, when Lena returned from the shop earlier than usual, she found her husband climbing the stairs to the hotel rooms accompanied by another woman. Lena produced her pistol as

The Shaffer Hotel in the late 1920s. *National Park Service.*

the mistress drew hers. Both shots went off wildly and missed their targets. The mistress's bullet found its way into the ceiling molding opposite the staircase, and Lena's bullet hit the ceiling behind the staircase. I can only imagine Pop's reaction during this tumultuous episode. However, there is no record of how it ended—except that it did not lead to a divorce. However, it was apparent that Pop was also quite the joker. In the *Albuquerque Journal* on January 24, 1984, Dewey Tidwell, a druggist in Mountainair in the early 1930s, recalled an incident that involved Pop Shaffer.

> *To say the least, things were never dull for long in Mountainair when I lived there. Being a closely knit little town, most everyone knew about the other fellow's activities or thought he did, and family disturbances often became the topic of discussion. For example, one time, Pop Shaffer and John Jackson decided to play jokes on their wives while the men were in Santa Fe attending the State Legislature.*
>
> *Knowing that Ma and Mrs. Jackson always suspected the worst of them when they were away from home, the two old boys gave birth to an idea they thought would be worth carrying out. One night, in their room at La Fonda in Santa Fe, Pop called Ma on the phone and, in a disguised voice, told her that he was a guest in a room next to Pop and John's. He told her that a wild party with women was happening in their room. John was squealing like a drunk woman, and Pop was kicking the furniture around to make the incident sound real.*

Ma immediately called Mrs. Jackson and got her out of bed, and soon, the two angry wives were on their way to Santa Fe, 120 miles to the north. When they arrived at the hotel, they proceeded to Pop and John's room, rapping loudly on the door and demanding admittance.

Both men were in their nightshirts. "What in the hell brings you two up here in the middle of the night?" Pop asked.

"Where's them women?" Mrs. Jackson asked as she jerked her husband from his bed. "We know you had a party here tonight."

Although they could not find any women in the room, the wives told the men in no uncertain terms to get dressed. The women were taking their husbands home. No amount of denying that they had consorted with women in their room convinced Ma and Mrs. Jackson of their husbands' innocence. Pop winked at John as if to say, "It was a damned good joke, no?" Both men were ready to go home anyway.

Shaffer died in 1964, and Lena, who ended up running the hotel when Shaffer became a full-time artist, died in 1978, shortly before the hotel was placed in the National Register of Historic Places.

The Shaffer Hotel in the 1930s. *National Park Service.*

The hotel then went through a series of owners, many from out of state, until it finally closed its doors without notice in May 2000. The Bank of Belen foreclosed on the property in the summer of 2001. The hotel was auctioned off on the steps of the Torrance County Courthouse in September that year, with the bank itself being the sole bidder and buying the property for resale.

Despite the hotel purchased in 2002 by a pair of antique dealers from California who hoped to renovate it, nothing much was done, and the hotel fell into disrepair. In 2004, Joel Marks purchased the hotel. He began a $1 million renovation that took the thirty original guest rooms down to nineteen, many with private bathrooms. The hotel reopened in December 2005. This is when the first published reports of hauntings at the hotel appeared.

Marks claimed that the east hallway upstairs was the most haunted part of the hotel, possibly, he speculated, because it is directly above the hand-painted ceiling of the restaurant to which Shaffer dedicated so much time. The hotel changed hands again in January 2011, when Emma Pack and her husband purchased the property. In a strange coincidence, their home in Willard burned down shortly after the purchase, much like the Shaffer's did in 1928.

One of the first newspaper articles that mentioned the ghosts of the hotel was published on January 23, 2006, in the *Albuquerque Journal*.

The lobby of the hotel in the late 1930s. *National Park Service.*

If staying in a historic hotel and possibly experiencing "spirited" encounters with friendly ghosts is your idea of a weekend getaway, the Shaffer Hotel in Mountainair might be what you're looking for. The Shaffer, owned by Joel Marks, is a historical 1920s landmark that Marks has poured his heart and soul—and more than $1 million—into restoring. He bought the hotel about two years ago. An Albuquerque native, Marks said that while riding his Harley-Davidson motorcycle through an area in the Manzano Mountains known as "The Loop," he stopped to have lunch in the restaurant that used to be inside the Shaffer Hotel. He was immediately overwhelmed with the atmosphere and the Pueblo Art Deco ceiling and said to himself, "This is pretty damned cool." After lunch, he went across the street to the Abo Trading Post and chatted with the clerk there about the hotel.

Handing her his business card, he said if it ever went up for sale, to let him know. Within two weeks, Marks received a call from a realtor that the Shaffer was on the market. Marks, who believes in such things, said it was just too much of a coincidence that the hotel was for sale in such a short time. He believes he was drawn to the hotel, as were his live-in managers, John and Karen Cate. Karen agrees with Marks that the hotel has a definite drawing power.

"Something called us here. This place has a special energy," she said. That "energy" might be the ghost of "Pop" Clem Shaffer—the first owner of the hotel. Pop Shaffer built the hotel in 1923 and poured himself into the building by personally painting the restaurant's ceiling and constructing a unique stone fence outside. Pop—and other ghosts—are said to still roam the hotel halls and occasionally play pranks on visitors.

The Shaffer has nineteen completely remodeled suites and rooms. Each is richly decorated and has antique furniture to add to the old Southwest atmosphere. Visitors can choose rooms ranging from a "cowboy" room, which has a single bed and uses a communal bathroom, to the "wedding suite," complete with two claw-foot tubs and a wet bar.

In 2005, Joel invited me and the Southwest Ghost Hunter's Association to the hotel to investigate the building. We have returned six times over the years, and the following are the ghost stories that are frequently told.

The first involves the cowboy rooms, which were very small areas with a single bed. Supposedly, they had been used by cowboys in the 1900s. On some occasions, the staff reported hearing noises and commotion coming from certain rooms in the hotel where there shouldn't have been anyone. When they searched inside the cowboy rooms, they found small footprints, which led them to believe that a deceased child, who had supposedly once lived in the area, was responsible for them. The tiny footprints would even appear on the rug, even though it had just been vacuumed. According to the staff, this occurs quite frequently. At first, they believed it to be nothing more than a hoax, so, out of precaution, they changed all the locks on the door, but the activity continued.

Another hotel employee told me her unusual story. She was once cleaning a freestanding, four-legged bathtub in one of the rooms. She thought about getting on top of the tub to clean the windows, as they were so dirty. Suddenly, an unseen voice shouted, "Don't do it!" She spun around but saw no one; the door was closed, and no one was in the room with her. In hindsight, she realized that if she had gotten up on the tub, she could have fallen out of the window, since most of the rooms were located on the second floor. Fortunately, she believes the ghost saved her by warning her not to do it. Now, she knows better than to stand up near a window without taking extra precautions.

Upstairs is a charming honeymoon suite. The room is larger than most and contains a king-sized bed and a fan to keep it cool. There are tasteful furnishings and an ornate armoire situated in the corner. People frequently remark on its beauty when they enter the room. It is large enough for clothes or whatever else one might need.

The ornately adorned ceiling of the restaurant. *Library of Congress.*

People have often sat on the bed and noticed an odd reflection in the armoire's mirror. They kept these stories to themselves until they went downstairs and told them to the staff. The person they described in the reflection was Mrs. Shaffer. It's something the staff has heard about many times over the years.

Another strange phenomenon occurs in the Jack and Jill room, which comprises rooms 17 and 18. This type of accommodation typically suggests that both rooms share a bathroom in the middle for convenience. Often, parents sleep in room 17, and their kids stay in room 18. That way, everyone has easy access to the restroom.

According to the story, in 1928, a cowboy found himself alone in one of the hotel rooms. Mountainair was known for its pinto bean production, and a cowboy had gone there to take part in an auction. Unfortunately, he ended up hanging himself in the bathroom. It's unclear why he was there or why nobody else was occupying the other room. All that is known for sure is that the cowboy hanged himself in the bathroom, and Pop Shaffer discovered him soon after. He looked at the guest registry to try and figure out who had stayed in that room—but curiously enough, no one had been registered for it.

The legend says that since Pop Shaffer and his staff couldn't figure out who this cowboy was or how to get in touch with his relatives, they buried him in a nearby public cemetery without putting down his name. They never found out who the cowboy was. However, as time passed, mysterious spirits and ghosts began appearing to people who stayed in those two rooms.

The first incident of this paranormal activity occurred with a visiting family. The father had heard the stories and shared some of the saga with his kids. He was very unconvinced that this ghost tale was true, so he decided to put it to the test by occupying room 18 while his children stayed in room 17. With an air of nonchalance, he mockingly challenged the spirit of the cowboy.

Anyway, the story goes that he dared the ghost to show itself. Nothing happened until later that night, when he got up to use the restroom. Suddenly, he was pinned against the wall by an unseen force. He called frantically for his kids, but they could not open the door, no matter how hard they tried. The invisible force eventually let him go, and he fell to the ground. When his kids were finally able to get in, they were terrified and wanted to leave immediately, only to find all of the doors locked. After much pleading from him, the ghost allowed them all to exit at 4:00 a.m. Descending the stairwell, they decided they wanted out and refused any refund. All they desired was to leave that place behind them and never return.

The fireplace in the lobby greets customers as they enter. *Photograph by the author.*

The artistic fence on the east side of the hotel adds a creepy ambiance to the hotel. *Library of Congress.*

The hotel in 2005. *Photograph by the author.*

There is another variant to this story, which is a little more docile. It claims that in the middle of the night, the man went to use the bathroom and felt a sudden chill. He turned to see the outline of a body on the bed. He attempted to go to his daughter's room but could not unlock its door. The children awoke and were likewise unable to open the door from their side. Early the following day, the woman who ran the front desk came in to find the man and his daughters sitting downstairs. The girls were crying. The man said they weren't staying another night and that the hotel could keep its money as far as he was concerned. The woman at the front desk said she made the refund anyway.

The location of the cowboy hanging story may be suspect, since before the remodel, there were only two bathrooms in the building. Hence, the shared bathroom between rooms 17 and 18 was most likely constructed during the 2005 remodel when eleven bathrooms were added to the hotel.

Yet another ghost story involves a room with a rocking chair that was constructed by Pop Shaffer. He made quite a few pieces of furniture for the hotel, and this particular piece is quite unique. It was said that a daughter, her mother and granddaughter had rented out the room before. They placed a suitcase on the rocking chair inside the room, and when they opened it, the suitcase suddenly shut itself abruptly. It startled them greatly, and other strange noises made them feel uneasy, but they managed to stay the entire night.

After years of increasing reports and complaints about odd occurrences involving the rocking chair, staff members removed it and placed it in storage in 2014. This was the solution, as all strange events ceased after its removal. The theory, of course, is that some ghosts had a particular affinity for the rocking chair and did not want anyone sitting in it or putting their belongings on it. This is why all the noise seemed to be focused on that one piece of furniture.

The Shaffer Hotel stands tall and proud, a testament to the history of Mountainair. Its facade is weather worn by the bright New Mexico sun but is well-maintained. The interior is equally charming, with antique furnishings and a dusty smell that hints at stories and secrets kept for years within its walls. If you are traveling anywhere near Mountainair, the Shaffer Hotel is a must-stop destination for anyone who loves a bit of history, charm and maybe a few ghosts in their lodgings.

9
THE VAL VERDE BATTLEFIELD

Lieutenant Colonel John Baylor led a small band of Texans to occupy the Mesilla Valley in 1861 and was soon joined by a three-thousand-man Confederate army under Brigadier General Henry Sibley. His goal was to capture Colorado and California, thus giving the Confederacy transcontinental recognition.

In early 1862, Sibley moved against Fort Craig in south-central New Mexico. The Union force of 1,250 regulars and 1,350 volunteers and militia was commanded by Colonel Edward Canby. When Canby refused to battle on the open plain south of the fort, Sibley retreated downriver to Paraje, crossing over to the east bank of the Rio Grande.

General Sibley thought it would take a single day for his army to reach the Valverde Ford, six miles away from Fort Craig. At that location, they could cross over the river again. However, the terrain was rugged and full of deep sand, which hindered their progress. By February 20, they'd still not arrived at the ford and were forced to make a dry camp for the evening.

Understanding that Sibley planned to reach the Valverde Ford, Canby sent a battery of cannons and two troops of volunteers to the other side of the river to deter the Texans. He organized his army into battle formation and directed skirmishers out front, but they were repulsed by Confederate artillery and gunfire. His first attempt at using a guided bomb was fruitless as well; it involved fitting explosives to a mule's back.

At dawn on Friday, February 21, 1862, Sibley sent Major Charles Pyron with 180 men to get a better look at the road to Val Verde. Hot on his heels was Major Henry Raguet and five other companies. As they made their

way north along the eastern edge of Black Mesa before curving around to head west along its northern border, they stumbled on a small cottonwood grove near the ford. There, Pyron found a line of Union cavalry waiting for them, and instantly, bullets began flying through the air. Canby quickly sent Colonel Benjamin Roberts with volunteers and regimental cavalry to help. When Major Raguet, Colonel William Scurry and the Fourth Regiment heard the gunfire, they galloped to the river to join the fight.

By 10:00 a.m., Captain Trevanion T. Teel's artillery had also arrived at the Val Verde ford. The Texans attempted to advance toward the river. However, they had to retreat due to a heavy Union artillery bombardment. Simultaneously, the Union forces moved upriver from Val Verde to encircle the Confederate right flank. This led Scurry to divide his forces and extend their line. On the Union's left side, Captain Alexander McRae began to fire on the Rebel position on the eastern bank with his artillery. By 11:00 a.m., the Rebels had retreated to a sandhill ridge east of the river. By midday, the Union army held the advantage.

It was one o'clock in the afternoon when General Sibley retired to an ambulance in the Confederate rear due to exhaustion and intoxication, leaving his army under the command of Colonel Thomas Green. At the same time, Captain Willis L. Lang led a company armed with lances in a brave yet

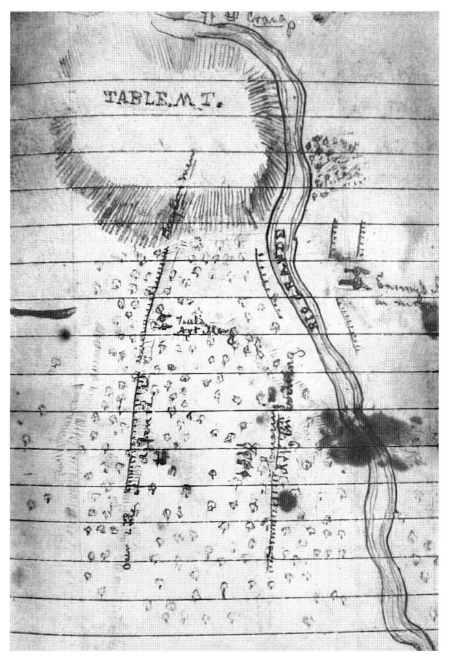

Opposite: A view of the Valverde Battlefield from on top of Black Mesa. *Photograph by the author.*

Above: A soldier's sketch of the Battle of Valverde. *Wikimedia Commons.*

suicidally dangerous attack against a group of New Mexican volunteers on the right flank of the Confederate forces. The federal line held their fire until the lancers were close enough and then let out a barrage that caused heavy losses for Company B of the Fifth Regiment. Captain Lang was severely wounded and later took his own life. At the same time, Lieutenant Demetrius M. Bass was also injured multiple times before he died just days later.

At three o'clock in the afternoon, Colonel Canby arrived on the battlefield and moved his right and center troops forward, with the left as a pivot. As this occurred, Green stealthily inched up on the Union center while Raguet's cavalry attacked the federal battery, taking shots at the Confederate left flank. After coming within one hundred yards of the Union weapons, they were eventually driven back. It was then that Green's advance on the right side became the tactical breakthrough of the fight. Despite McRae's forces pelting grapeshot at them, the Rebels rushed on the Union artillery with brutal ferocity. In scarcely more than eight minutes, it was all over: McRae and half of his soldiers had been wiped out at their guns, and 80 percent of all the men killed or wounded in the fray fell near or around McRae's battery.

The Union line fell apart, and their troops scattered, many throwing away their weapons as they ran. Many died trying to get across the Rio Grande. Colonel Canby sent a white flag toward the Rebel forces, asking only for an end to fighting so that the federals could recover their dead and wounded without being put in harm's way. The Union side suffered 222 casualties, while the Confederates lost 183. The next day, the Confederate soldiers were buried in blankets in trenches; those on the Union side were interred at Fort Craig.

The Confederates won the battle, though it cost them dearly, with 36 dead, 150 wounded and 1 missing out of 2,590 men. They could not breach the fort's walls, so instead of trying to capture it, they moved forward on their mission to collect supplies in Albuquerque and Santa Fe. Thus, they left the battlefield in Union hands.

Considering himself outnumbered, Canby chose not to pursue Sibley and instead sent mounted attachments of New Mexico volunteers against the confederate's rear for harassment. He remained with the main body at Fort Craig to cut off the Confederate supply line and to intercept reinforcements for Sibley, eventually hoping to pin the Confederates between himself and Union reinforcements from Fort Union.

After the Civil War ended, Fort Craig and the Val Verde Battlefield were left for the New Mexico plains to swallow up again. However, despite its remoteness, there are multiple claims that the old battlefield is haunted by the spirits of the soldiers who died there.

I was drinking a beer at the Val Verde Hotel in Socorro when I heard about the haunted battlefield from someone at the bar. Knowing I was investigating the building, the bartender told me there was a cowboy who had some ghost stories that could interest me. So, after buying him a beer, I sat down with him, and he told me his story.

The cowboy was an employee of the Armendaris Ranch. This vast 362,885-acre ranch lies in south-central New Mexico along the Rio Grande River. Here is his story.

The sun blazed down on me as I rode west toward the river, eager to enjoy my day off. The horse snorted nervously, and I tightened my grip on the reins, not wanting to startle it. As we crossed the water, I noticed a man in a tattered Confederate uniform standing in the shadows of the riverbank. He stepped into view, and I got a better look at him—only then did I realize he had no head! I gasped and instinctively kicked my horse forward as a gunshot rang out. My heart pounding, I bent low over the horse's neck as we galloped away. Breathless and shaking, I finally slowed the horse down to a trot. I turned around to make sure I was far enough away from the river and the headless Confederate soldier. But as I looked back, I saw no one.

A strange image captured by ghost hunters while visiting the battlefield. *Photograph courtesy of the Southwest Ghost Hunters.*

A reenactment of the Battle of Valverde, near Socorro. *Photograph by the author.*

> *As I rode back, I couldn't shake the image of the headless Confederate soldier from my mind. I had heard rumors of a Civil War battle that had taken place near the Armendaris Ranch, but I had never given it much thought before. Now, I couldn't help but wonder if the soldier's ghost was somehow connected to that battle.*

Another eyewitness account was received six months later in an email from someone who claimed to be an engineer working for the Burlington Northern Santa Fe Railway. He spoke of his journey heading north and said he witnessed what seemed like a full-on charge by a reenactment group as he passed through a battlefield. However, there was no audience around to witness this spectacle. It wasn't until later that he discovered reenactments were never performed in that area, and given that ranch hands patrolled the region, the men he saw couldn't have been anyone living. The hair on the back of his neck stood up as he recounted the sight, and even though he knew it defied explanation, he couldn't shake off the feeling that something otherworldly had transpired.

Are the ghosts real? Who can say for sure? What we do know is that the Civil War and its tragic fatalities provide plenty of inspiration for some amazing ghostly tales.

10
THE GHOST OF SCARLETT

From 1880 to 1915, Albuquerque became a place where women could legally engage in sex work. They did this in brothels, which were one-room operations, and on the street. The original red-light district was located near the current-day Old Town Plaza.

The women in Old Town Albuquerque weren't as flashy or flamboyant as those of Denver's "demimonde." They wore Japanese-style kimonos with burning incense sticks called punk in their hair or more conservative dresses known as "Mother Hubbard's" at restaurants and saloons. Unlike the ladies of Denver, they did not show much skin.

In between customers, the girls would often guzzle down alcohol and wind up getting into arguments with one another. The newspapers loved to cover these quarrels, since they usually involved the female workers of the establishment. On July 30, 1885, the *Albuquerque Journal* noted:

> *Marshal Ostrander's attention is called to the noisy female loafers who congregate in and around the dance hall. About three times a week, several of these "soiled by inclination, fill up with tarantula juice and make night hideous by their pugilistic tendency to fight and scratch among themselves."*

In 1881, a peculiar altercation between two inhabitants of Old Town's underworld took place in a dance hall that served as a cover for a brothel. The *Journal* reported on December 6 that year:

At an early hour last night, two women named respectively Georgie Smith, Busy Sharon Johnson, and Maud Eddie were in Sim Ovelin's dance hall. They were not on good terms with each other, and soon, they were disputing and quarreling. Miss Smith, who is a great big six-footer, drew a little pistol, about the size of a pea shooter, from her pocket and blazed away at her enemy. The ball hit the girl's side but struck her corset steel and glanced off without doing any harm except to barely break the skin. Georgie skipped, and the matter was hushed up without any arrests being made.

In fact, Old Town was such a hotbed of sex work and violence in the late 1800s that it sparked a public outcry in the local newspapers, such as this one recorded by the *Albuquerque Citizen* on December 20, 1898.

"Murderer's Corral" should be the appellation of the location in the old town of Albuquerque where the murder took place last night. Instead of "Fighting Corral," by which name it has been known for half a century. The killing last night is the second at the same Martinez wine shop within a year. The "vinata" is in a very unsavory neighborhood. There are a few, very few, decent families in the vicinity. Over the way from the scene of the murder is probably the worst dive in New Mexico. Its proprietors began in a small, modest (?) way—a little music, a little wine, a little something else. Now, they own a great cooperative establishment consisting of a store, restaurant, wine rooms, lodgings with or without companions, harem, etc. Rumors of knock-out drops, rolling of railroad men and others are frequent; also, of innocent girls seduced to lives of debauchery. This beastly concern is within 300 or 400 feet of a public school and is also about that distance from a temple of religious worship. It cannot but taint the morals of children whose minds are so receptive. Outside of the notorious concern are many smaller ones near the scene of the murder. Here herd promiscuously together the most depraved of both sexes and in the more pretentious establishment are bred the crimes of night and the shocking exhibits so often witnessed by day in the streets in that part of the town—the town noted all over Spanish America in the days that are gone for its culture and refinement. Alas! Albuquerque, the old! That the misdoings, the unpunished misdoings of a few, should have bedraggled your fair fame in these later days! Capital flees from your doors and decency from many of your portals.

On top of their personal battles, the girls had to deal with a host of other issues, including rough men, unhappy clients and problematic lovers. An

Old Town Albuquerque in 1888. *Utah Department of Cultural and Community Engagement, 1888–1912.*

article appeared in the *Albuquerque Citizen* in 1899 about such an event that would prove to be intriguing.

> *Yesterday morning, at 11 o'clock, Lottie McDonald, one of New Town's soiled doves who has recently taken up her residence in the "alley" of Old Town, received quite a severe beating from her lover, Bill Whitney, the hack driver. Complaint was filed before Justice Beterino Crollott, and late in the afternoon ay Sheriff Smith arrested Whitney on this side. This morning, the woman beater was fined $20 and costs, or twenty-five days, in the county jail. He went to jail.*

What makes this article interesting is that it mentions "the alley." This part of Old Town is south of James Street (now South Plaza Street), where many brothels were located. Locals whisper of a horrifying specter that haunts this area, known only as "Scarlett." Her presence lingers in the air like a chill, as if she is always watching with her pale and haunting countenance.

The employees at Casa de Fiesta restaurant had a chilling tale to share in 1997, and it was the first story I have heard about her. The employees told tales of a spectral woman in the alleyway with flaming red hair and a dark blue or purple dress. Though they were scared to talk to her, they felt her presence as she moved silently through the storage rooms at the back of the restaurant, rearranging objects on shelves with an invisible force. When approached, she quickly disappeared into thin air, leaving a lingering chill long after she was gone. Stranger still, the eerie figure materialized in broad daylight, an unnerving sight that sent shivers up the spines of those who witnessed it. Every detail of its presence was burned into their minds with a terrorizing clarity, and they could only stare in disbelief as the mysterious vision stood before them.

Several employees of the La Placita Restaurant across the street swear they have seen the mysterious figure at the end of the alley. Initially, they thought she was an unhoused person and called social services to provide aid, yet the authorities were of no help. Then, one afternoon, a brave waitress determined to make a difference approached the stranger with an offering of food, only to watch in disbelief as Scarlett moved farther back up the alley and disappeared. With heightened suspicion, whispers spread—perhaps there is something more to these tales than anyone can imagine.

In 2001, I did an interview on a local radio show. Several people contacted me through email with their stories, but one stood out. A man named Eddie, who had been listening that morning, mentioned seeing a strange woman in the alley behind South Plaza Street and was sure he had just seen a ghost.

The apparition is most often spotted from this corner. *Photograph by the author.*

We agreed to meet in Old Town, where Eddie told his story and led me to where he saw the ghost. This is his account.

My girlfriend and I had just finished lunch in Old Town when she stopped to admire a window display at the Old Town Emporium. I remained outside, determined to have one last cigarette before we drove off. Despite my attempts to hide my addiction from her and not allow it to become a part of our relationship, I pulled out my lighter with eagerness. She knew that I had one every now and then, so surely, she wouldn't object. With every spark of the flint wheel came another wave of disappointment as it soon became clear that no butane was left. In frustration, I threw the lighter away and cursed for having to wait what would feel like an eternity until I could get another smoke.

I peered intently down the alley and saw a woman leaning against the wall, her face smothered in shadows. She was slowly releasing wispy tendrils of smoke from her lips, and I could make out the faint glint of embers emanating from her cigarette. Assuming she held my only hope for lighting up my own smoke, I started down the alley cautiously, my eyes darting around for any other smokers hanging out nearby before I moved on. There were none, so I continued on.

My heart pounded as I stepped closer to her, my voice shaking as I asked if she had a light. She didn't move an inch, and it seemed like she hadn't heard me. I was only twenty feet or so away from her when, suddenly, the shout of my girlfriend reverberated down the alley like thunder.

"Eddie! What are you doing?"

I spun on my heels and screamed at her that I'd only be gone a minute. When I looked back, the woman had vanished without a trace—no footprints, no path to follow, no evidence of where she could have gone. It was as if she evaporated into nothingness.

Eddie described the woman as having messy red hair that looked like it hadn't been washed in several days. Her purple dress was tied in a knot at the waist, and her skin was harsh and weathered. "She was very ordinary looking. There was nothing about her that really stood out to me upon approaching her."

Six months later, another sighting of the strange woman lurking in the alley was reported to the ghost hunters. This time, she manifested before a man who was walking with his wife on San Felipe Street after parking their car. He had just lit a cigarette while discussing where to go for lunch.

Looking down the "alley" late at night. This area was once the main passage to access the brothels and wine rooms in Old Town during the roaring 1880s. *Photograph by the author.*

As they passed by the alley, the husband glanced over and saw a woman leaning against the wall "about halfway" down the alley. He said that the strange woman was also smoking, and she motioned for him to come over. He felt a chill run down his spine and quickly turned to his wife, grabbing her hand and urging her to hurry along. But as they walked past the alley, he couldn't help but glance back over his shoulder, his curiosity piqued. What she did next shocked him.

> She waved at me again and then grabbed the top of her dress and pulled it to the side, exposing one of her breasts. I freaked out, as my wife was right beside me. So, I ignored her and continued walking, wondering what kind of place we were walking into.

The couple finally ate lunch at a local café and heard about the Old Town ghost tour. Intrigued by the stories they had heard, they decided to sign up for the tour that evening. Walking through Old Town, they listened intently to the guide's tales of restless spirits and unexplained phenomena.

When they reached the alley where the woman had appeared, the guide paused and told them the story of the woman in the purple dress. At the time, it was a "bonus" story that the guides would tell occasionally, as not much was known about her. The man then realized he had encountered the same woman earlier that day. After the tour was finished, he told his story to the tour guide.

Soon, with more stories, Scarlett became another stop on the ghost tour of Old Town. In the early days of the ghost tour, the tour guides were ghost hunters and often received emails from guests about their experiences in Old Town.

After dining at La Placita in Old Town, my husband and I were walking back to the car, which was parked in the parking lot adjoining Central Street. As we passed the alleyway behind South Plaza Street, we heard a sobbing sound coming from the far end of the alley. There was a woman down at the other end who was frantically pacing back and forth. I could tell that she was a redhead and wore a long dress that was either dark blue or purple. The sobbing sound was coming from her direction.

My husband, Andrew, decided that whatever was happening was not our business, so we continued to the car. Once we arrived at the parking lot, Andrew changed his mind and decided to go back and check on the poor woman we saw in the alley. Not wanting to be left alone in the car, I went along with him.

We took a shortcut from the parking lot between two houses and entered the alley, only to find that the woman was gone. Relieved that we did not have to deal with it, I turned to leave when my husband called out to me. He was looking at the footprints left in the freshly fallen snow. Clearly visible were the impressions of a lady's high-heeled shoe. From the look of the tracks, it appeared that she had paced back and forth over a 15-foot area several times. I saw nothing interesting about it until Andrew pointed out a very strange fact. There were no footprints leading to or away from the "pacing" footprints, so how did this woman get there and leave without leaving any tracks. Maybe we saw one of the ghosts that was mentioned on the ghost tour.

However, there are pros and cons of having ghost hunters as tour guides. New sightings added up quickly, and this made tours more exciting. Ghost hunters brought their knowledge of the paranormal and folklore to life, giving guests an unparalleled experience. Unfortunately, as the tours were ninety minutes long, the more recent ghost stories replaced the older ones, erasing historic sightings from the narrative. Worse still, some stories were added before investigations had been completed, creating historical inaccuracies.

One such error manifested at a historic building in Old Town, the Manual Springer House (now the Covered Wagon), which was rumored to have been a brothel and eventual speakeasy during Prohibition. Legend has it that Scarlet got into a fight with a coworker at the location and died. Thus, she now haunts the building.

The book *Old Town, Albuquerque, New Mexico: A Guide to Its History and Architecture* by Byron A. Johnson states that "Springer died in 1917, and according to Old Town tradition, the house was a speakeasy and brothel during prohibition." An article published by the *Albuquerque Journal* on October 31, 1926, confirms this.

> The "Springer House," a few doors west of "Zamora's Place," is an attractive two-story brick building, with a screened-in porch. It is directly across from the church and only half a block from the Old Town public school. Besides the parlors there is a dancing room, with an electric piano, the floor of the room laid with linoleum. Here and there in the parlors are several floor and table lamps. The resort boasted of nearly half a dozen girls, and those on an off night in a bad week. Beer was served for drinks at 30 cents a small glass.

However, the knife fight that supposedly ended Scarlett's life is absent from the newspapers and comes from secondhand accounts. Because of this, I lean more toward the version that sets Scarlett in the latter part of the nineteenth century.

The place where she has been seen is the same area that used to house one of the most notorious brothels in Old Town, run by Madam Rumalda Griego. At least twice, the Bernalillo County Court called Griego in on charges of causing public nuisance. In an 1882 court casebook kept by the New Mexico State Archives and Records Center, the judge's remarks and witnesses' accounts of her activities can still be found.

> The Territory vs. Rumalda Griego
> (Maintaining a Public Nuisance)
>
> Cornelius D. Murphy was deputy of the sheriff in 1882. Know defendant. She lived in [illegible] alley in this town. She kept a wine room and kept

women there. I do not know why she kept them there. Went there in my official capacity. Went to arrest parties who were fighting there often. She had beds and bedsteads, a good many of them. 2 or 3 rooms with beds in them. There was more than one bed in each room. She was a single woman. The women were not her children or related to her. People said the women were prostitutes. They lodged there. Some of the men were bad and some good. They drank and used bad language, and the women sat in their laps. Have seen these men and women in bed together. I knew the names of the girls there. I knew what the reputation was.

Harry Richmond (former law officer). Lives in Albuquerque and did prior to October 17, 1882. Know defendant. She lived on the south side of Old Town in an alley. I was in her house several times prior to Oct. She had a wine room there, and I have been called in to stop disturbances there. Women were there drinking with the men. The reputation of the women there was that of prostitutes. Men drank beer or wine with the women. Women in their laps. Heard obscene and indecent language there. Have been called in to quell disturbances there and arrest people for disorderly conduct.
Verdict Guilty
Fine of $75 & Costs

It's essential to note that the moniker "Scarlett" is just a label for the ghost. There is no knowledge of who she truly was. Nevertheless, this has not halted people from guessing her real identity.

Following my writing of *The Ghosts of Old Town Albuquerque*, I explored the records to discover any woman in Old Town that was rumored or thought to have been a sex worker who met an untimely end. Utilizing what is known about "Scarlett's" physical traits and other facts, there is a wide range of potential culprits.

The first was a woman simply called Minnie. Her death was documented in the *Albuquerque Journal* on January 20, 1883.

A woman of the town, who was known by the name of Minnie, died in the west end last night of consumption, hastened by an attack of varioloid. She was entirely destitute, and her burial expenses were soon subscribed by the demi-monde.

The problem with this guess is that we have no descriptions of the woman. Thus, this one is simply speculative based on the fact that she was a sex worker who died in Old Town.

The next story of a soiled dove who passed away in Old Town was printed in the *Albuquerque Morning Journal* on January 14, 1910.

> *Adela Chavez, for a number of years a character in the various redlight districts throughout the territory, died sometime early yesterday morning as the result of an overdose of morphine. The woman's body was found at 7 o'clock yesterday morning in a room in "Tom's Place." in Old Town, where she had been an inmate for several months past. According to evidence brought out at the coroner's inquest yesterday, the woman had threatened to kill herself a number of times recently but had put off the deed until the arrival of Monica Aranda of Belen, whom she claimed was her husband. Aranda arrived in Albuquerque Wednesday morning and was with the Chavez woman Wednesday night. The coroner's jury returned a verdict to the effect that death was caused by morphine administered by the woman herself. Aranda and the Chavez woman conducted an establishment in Willard about two years ago, which was destroyed by fire, money and jewels belonging to the Chavez woman, valued at $3,000, being consumed.*
>
> *The body of the unfortunate woman was removed yesterday to Borders' undertaking establishment. It will be shipped to Belen this morning, where internment will be made.*

Tom's place is now the Gold Star Saloon, which was once located diagonally across the street from the old Bernalillo County Court House, about where the Old Albuquerque Post Office on Central SW stands today. The problem with assuming Adela is the phantom figure is that there is no description of her, and the location of her death is wrong, making it a somewhat shaky conclusion.

Finally, I found another death that matched the proper location. Though this is an educated guess, it appears to be most likely based on available evidence. The backstory that led to her untimely demise was published in the *Albuquerque Morning Journal* on January 17, 1881.

> *In a low extension in the rear of Armstrong's saloon, on the west side of the plaza, live two soiled doves, who revel and debauch under the euphonious names of "Belle" and "Maud." They are both apparently possessed of refined and cultured literary tastes, and delight to spend their leisure hours, which are many, pouring over the pages of a ten-cent novel and imbibing tales of blood and thunder on the borders. Of late, however, a marked*

Old Town in 1908. The building to the left was the location of Armstrong's Saloon. In an extension behind this building were a pair of cribs inhabited by two soiled doves, Belle and Maud. *Library of Congress.*

change has come over the literary cravings and consequently over the life and prospects of these fair damsels.

A few weeks ago, they got ahold of a novel by May Agnes Fleming. This was a work of an entirely different character from anything they had before read. It told of pure lives and glorious rewards and let in such a flood of light on their own blighted lives that they concluded and mutually agreed that the latter were not worth living. It would seem that Belle came to this conclusion first, and without consulting her friend and co-laborer, acted on it by swallowing a large dose of laudanum, with intent to "lay down to rest," but the dose was only sufficient to make Belle very sick, and a restorative promptly administered soon brought her back to her usual health of body, but the buoyant spirit that was won't cheer the hearts of her friends and callers ne'er returned. This was about a week ago.

On yesterday evening, the two friends sat together alone in their den and discussed life and death in all their relations and phrases, and then and

103

there mutually agreed to "shake off this mortal coil," to give this corruption a show, to quit this vile den of lust and hatred, and fly away on snowy wings to the everlasting temple of purity and love. Acting on this agreement they repaired to the drug store of F.H. Kent and there purchased an ounce phial, filled with a fluid labeled "Tr. Opii." The contents of this they were to divide in equal parts and swallow half at the same moment. This was very well planned, but it seems doubtful whether or not the festive Maud was acting in good faith with her more melancholy and earnest friend, Belle.

On returning from the druggist, they sat talking and arranging the preliminaries of a double funeral, at which both were to be present, without fail, when a young man, who loves best the society of Miss Maud, entered. The latter forgot at once all about the other little affair and set herself about entertaining her lover. Belle was not interested in small talk and other trifles of this vain world and called to her friend to "pay her vow to the Most High," at the same time dashing off half of the contents of the fatal fluid.

Maud paid little attention to this proceeding and sat chatting gaily to her lover until the book, which Belle was trying to read, dropped from her fingers. The young man suggested that it might be well to call in a doctor, but Maud thought differently, as she was satisfied that her friend wanted to die, and this would undoubtedly have been the final result had not Belle's lover appeared on the scene. He took in the situation at a glance and hastened to summon Dr. A.H. Ashley, who, when he arrived, found Belle pretty far gone. But the doctor was equal to the emergency, and prompt action brought the patient back to life after a few hours. She is still in critical condition but, with careful nursing, will recover.

Eventually, Belle was back on her feet, and by 1882, she was employed at Madam Rumalda Griego's wine room in the "alley" of Old Town. It was here that she finally succeeded in taking her own life with her third suicide attempt.

Belle's time in the wine room was marked by her reckless behavior and her unabashed embrace of the seedier aspects of life. Her lovers came and went, but none of them ever truly understood her. The pain of her past haunted her every waking moment, and she found solace in the bottom of a bottle of laudanum.

11

THE PINK LADY

The early days of New Albuquerque saw a rush of activity, as it was populated mainly by railroad workers, cowboys, merchants and miners. As these men worked almost constantly for at least ten hours each day, there were plenty of saloons and red-light districts to serve them. Between 1880, when the railroad arrived, and 1885, when the town was incorporated, more than one hundred saloons popped up around Railroad Avenue (now Central Avenue) and its side streets.

At the northern end of town was the entertainment district comprising "gilded dens of vice" and their smaller counterparts, the cribs. At least five notorious pleasure palaces were in operation, with names like the Cottage, Rose Cottage and Nora's. The insides of these single- or two-story wooden buildings were luxuriously decorated with red, plush parlor sets, Brussel carpets, marble-topped tables and numerous mirrors. However, fighting among the working girls and their customers soon gave this part of Albuquerque a new nickname, Hell's Half Acre.

In addition to personal warfare, the girls had considerable trouble with each other, dissatisfied customers and their boyfriends. On occasion, this would lead to a suicide or even murder. One such incident occurred on September 12, 1893. It made the headlines in the *Albuquerque Journal* with the title "BRUTAL MURDER."

Saturday evening, Alcaria Baca, a young woman of ill fame, was found murdered in her room in the alley between Copper and Railroad Avenues and Third and Fourth Streets. Her room was the western one of the three-room adobe building on the south side of the alley. The body, in a nightgown, lay on the floor in a pool of blood, the skull fractured with a rock, and the throat cut and hacked from ear to ear. The bloody knife, a common six-inch bladed dull butcher knife, lay near the hip, and the blood-stained rock was found within two feet of the lifeless body. The electric light was still burning in the room. The dressing-case and trunk bore evidence of having been rummaged, the till of the trunk laying disordered on the bed. The earrings and finger ring usually worn by the woman were missing. Everything pointed to robbery as the motive, else the murderer made a very clever effort to cover up his tracks. The theory of robbery is sustained by the fact that a woman in the same vicinity was recently robbed of almost $150.

Yesterday, a coroner's jury empaneled by Judge Burke investigated the cause of death, but the testimony elicited failed to throw any light on the subject. Marshal Dodd and his police force worked hard to bring in all the evidence obtainable, and Mayor Field was present and conducted a searching examination of the witnesses in person.

Suspicion rested that Celestino Pasquanelli, the murdered woman's lover, knew more about the case than he cared to divulge, and the drift of the examination was in that direction. The testimony concluded. Mayor Field stated that, in his opinion, the evidence at hand did not warrant a verdict, fastening suspicion on any known person, but that the jury could find as it pleased. The main points in the evidence are as follows:

Dr Hope described the wounds and said the fracture of the skull inflicted by the rock was sufficient in itself to produce death. He advanced the theory that the victim, after having been brained with the rock, which weighed about two pounds, might have been making some noise, which led the murderer to cut her throat. The knife was the one used by the woman in her room.

Jennie Clifford occupies the adjoining room to the one occupied by the deceased. She saw the deceased about one o'clock Sunday morning. About 10 or fifteen minutes after the alarm of fire at the Weiller & Anderson store, which was about three o'clock of that morning, she heard a rap at the door of deceased and heard the murdered woman invite the visitor in. They talked in the woman's language. Shortly afterward, she heard her scream, "Oh my God!" She got up and went to the window and saw a man going away. It was dark, and hence, she could not describe the man. She did not suspect a murder was committed and returned to bed. She got up at 3 o'clock that afternoon and asked the other women in the row if *they had seen the deceased and finally told the circumstances to Officer Fornoff. A tall Mexican gambler habitually visited the deceased as did also the Italian, Pasquanelli. The deceased was not supposed to have any money.*

Blanch Wilson saw the deceased the night previous, heard the subdued scream and then heard someone running away.

Celestino Pasquanelli was placed on the stand. He had known the deceased familiarly about two years; saw the deceased alone last time about 9 o'clock Saturday night when he called at her room, but did not go in. Heard of the murder from Pietrini, his partner, who works at the Atlantic & Pacific shop.

Witness has charge of the Bambini lodging house; the deceased came to him Saturday noon at the lodging house; witness denied having quarreled with her and having refused her something to eat. She was not drunk but was drinking the day previous. He had none of her money, and she did not give him any money to put in the bank for her. I have no money in the bank.

Mr. Bacheci owns the furniture in her room; he was with Pasquanelli Saturday night until about 11:30 o'clock, went to bed about 12 o'clock, got up and went to the fire, and returned to bed. He went to the deceased's room Sunday afternoon at about 2 o'clock, but there was no response to a rap on the door, and he went away. His partner, Pietrini, corroborated the testimony of Pasquanelli as to his movements on Saturday night.

Lulu Giardia testified: "I was with the deceased all day Saturday and had supper with her; the deceased was drinking but not drunk. The deceased went to Pasquanelli's lodging house to clean rooms. When she came back, she said he would not give her anything to eat. I went with the deceased to her room Saturday night, almost 12:00 o'clock; while there, the deceased lover came and talked one side with the deceased. I think it was Pasquanelli. The deceased told me that she had money in the bank with Pasquanelli."

Miss Chambers, who rooms at the Bambini lodging house, testified to seeing Pasquanelli leaving his room to go to the fire. He was dressed and was putting on his coat as he was going out.

Lilly St. Clair saw the deceased at half past two o'clock Sunday morning; she was sitting in a rocking chair in her room. The witness next saw her when she pulled back the window screen Sunday evening with a whip handle and beheld the body lying on the floor.

The jury, accompanied by Major Field, visited the scene of the tragedy in an effort to arrive at a satisfactory theory of the murder. The jury returned the following verdict:

"We, the undersigned, justice of the pence and coroner's jury, find that the deceased, Alcaria Bacs, came to her death from blows on the head and wounds inflicted in the throat with a knife by party or parties to us unknown."

Alcaria's murder was never solved, and her killer was never brought to justice. As for her lover, he was murdered seven months later. According to the *Santa Fe New Mexican* from April 20, 1894,

In the district court at Albuquerque, Miguel Morelli was yesterday found guilty of murder in the second degree. He killed Celestino Pasquanelli.

In the years following Alcaria's death, murmurs of a ghost roaming the alley began to surface. Vague stories circulated about a stalwart female specter draped in a light pink nightgown, surfacing from the shadows to haunt the alley by garbage bins during the predawn hours. People also reported hearing eerie voices emanating from the pitch-black alleyway and doors slamming shut, and they smelled an overpowering perfume scent. Others have claimed to have seen ethereal shadows lingering in the air, a sensation of being monitored and hearing spectral footsteps thumping against the pavement. As if to add further terror to this ghostly tale, some even claimed to have heard a female voice whispering warnings or secrets into their ears while they walked past late at night.

There have also been reports of a dark figure suddenly emerging from the shadows, darting across the street in front of oncoming cars. Drivers slam on their brakes, screeching to a stop as they see the blur rush by, but they find no one when they search for what they thought was a person. Yet an eerie stillness lingers in the air.

One evening, a woman named Monica told me of her strange experience with the ghost during a book signing. She and her husband were walking back to their room at the Clyde Hotel after dining at Tucanos Brazilian Grill.

As they passed by the alley, Monica couldn't shake off the feeling of being watched, like a pair of eyes were following their every move. Suddenly, a gust of wind blew past them, carrying the overpowering scent of perfume. Monica's husband shrugged it off, but she knew it was something more, something that wasn't quite right. As they continued walking, Monica couldn't help but feel as if something was tugging at her, pulling her toward the alleyway.

Against her better judgment, Monica followed the pull. She stopped and turned to look down the alley. That's when someone or something whispered in her ear.

"Don't trust him," the voice breathed, sending chills down Monica's spine. She spun around, but there was no one there, just the empty alleyway and the flickering streetlights.

Monica's heart raced as she quickly caught up with her husband. She couldn't shake off the feeling of foreboding, the sense that something was terribly wrong. Her mind raced with questions and doubts, but she kept silent, afraid of being ridiculed by her husband.

Another story was told to me by a couple who decided to wander around Third and Copper Streets, the old red-light district, after attending the Albucreepy Ghost Walk. They turned south at Fourth Street and headed back toward Central Avenue when they passed the alley.

The woman felt a sudden coldness as they walked by, like they had entered another realm. Her husband brushed it off as nerves from the ghost stories they had just heard, but she couldn't shake off the feeling that something was watching them.

They walked a few more steps before they heard the sound of footsteps behind them. They turned around, but no one was there. The footsteps continued, getting louder and closer. Suddenly, they heard a voice whisper, "Help me."

The couple froze, unsure of what to do. Although the voice sounded like it was coming from the alley, it could have been coming from Central Avenue, muffled by the traffic noise. Then the voice whispered again, "Please, help me."

They followed the sound of the voice, and it led them down the deserted alley. The couple cautiously walked down the alley, their eyes scanning the surroundings. They couldn't see anyone or anything out of the ordinary. Suddenly, they heard the voice again, this time louder and more desperate. "Please, help me!" it cried out.

The woman's heart raced with fear and compassion. She wanted to help whoever was calling out for help, but her husband was hesitant. He didn't want to get involved in something potentially dangerous. However, the woman couldn't ignore the plea for help. She moved toward a dumpster, where the voice seemed to be coming from, but no one was there. Yet a faint trace of perfume floated in the air. However, her husband had had enough and insisted that they leave. Still not seeing anyone, the woman agreed. "It was such a strange experience," she told me. "I don't think that I will ever forget it."

Most of the strange phenomena occur in September, which leads some local ghosthunters to search to discover the ghost's identity. But is it really the restless spirit of Alcaria Baca?

The dank alley behind Knockouts Gentlemen's Club carries a strange and sinister air, as if the walls themselves know of the strange phenomena that occur there. It seems drawn to this spot like a moth to a flame. Oddly enough, it is here where this eerie event is most frequently witnessed.

Because of this, it is often assumed that the ghost was nothing more than one of the dancers of the establishment or perhaps an unfortunate unhoused person searching through the garbage bins. However, some think the spirit of a young woman in pink haunts the alleyway, doomed to roam the place of her death.

12

THE PAINTED LADY BED AND BREW

The Painted Lady's history is full of obscurity and tales of legend. Its construction dates to 1881, leaving a legacy of renowned brawls and shootouts. It was first noted on the Sanborn Fire Insurance Map in 1900 and reportedly run by Cesario "Sario" Gonzales. Accounts of violence erupted, such as this one reported in the *Albuquerque Journal* on August 19, 1912.

> *As the result of a half-drunken brawl which took place yesterday afternoon near the sawmill north of town, Miguel Sedillo lies this morning at the point of death, and he and three others are prisoners in the county jail.*
>
> *The fight occurred just outside the Swastika Saloon, near the entrance to the mill properties of Twelfth Street and the sawmill road and is said to have started inside the resort. Sedillo and his brother, Celso, were the participants on one side, and Sidiaco Guerrero and Juan Calderon, two natives of Mexico, were their opponents. No one seems to know just how the battle began. It is claimed that the men were all in the saloon and were all partly drunk, that they started a fight, and that "Si" Gonzalez, proprietor of the place, ejected them.*
>
> *A deputy sheriff, Ramon D. Ortiz, had passed along that way but a few minutes before, and bystanders who saw the injured man, called to him. He arrested the whole quartet and took them to the county jail in Old Albuquerque. Ortiz's action was very prompt, and it is due to him that the two Mexico natives did not get away. They were washing away the stains of the fray in a house nearby when he arrested them.*

The business card of the Swastika Saloon. *Image courtesy of the Painted Lady Bed and Brew.*

Miguel Sedillo is barely alive. He almost died yesterday afternoon while being treated by Dr. C.A. Frank, county physician, at the jail. He was kept there last night because the doctor feared to have him moved to the hospital. Sedillo is gashed through the neck and about the head. He lost large quantities of blood before medical attendance could be obtained, and if he recovers from his wounds, will demonstrate more than ordinary vitality. For some minutes, the doctor had to work to merely keep him alive before he could stitch up the gashes.

Celso Sedillo is cut about the face and hands. Juan Calderon is gashed over the eyebrow. Sidiaco Guerrero was not cut but was knocked down and kicked. He may develop serious internal injuries. Ortiz, who made the arrest, tells his story as follows:

"I was passing along the sawmill road when the people there called to me that a man had been cut. I looked back and saw two men in the road. They were the Sedillos. I had two men watch them and went into a room occupied by Francisco and Jinio Mendez, where the other two were washing up, and arrested them. Then I got a hack and took the whole four to the jail.

"The witnesses were two women, Manuelita Garcia and Carolina Valder. They saw it all."

A long search failed to reveal the two women who live near the mill. Search also failed to discover the whereabouts of the Mendez brothers, who left their room just as it was when the arrest was made. A pan of soapy water wagged on a chair. A cake of soap lay beside it, and there were blood stains everywhere. There was no sign of either of the occupants, however.

All three of the men in jail who were able to talk refused absolutely to say a word about the affray. They maintained a complete silence, and it will likely be some time before the real cause of the fight is forthcoming. Ortiz said that when arrested, all four of the men were sober, which fails to jibe with the story that they had been drinking.

Miguel Sedillo has appeared in similar affrays several times before, it is alleged, and bears an evil reputation in police circles. He has been in the penitentiary for cutting up other men and, when last tried for that offense, committed a second similar one before a jury could be secured to try him on the first charge. The other Sedillo recently completed an eleven-month term in jail.

The two Mexico natives are said to be rough characters but have been in no actual trouble here before. They live near the Summer Garden, at Mountain Road and Fourteenth Street. The Sedillos live near the Indian school. They work wherever they can at odd jobs and the like. The other two have worked for the American Lumber Company.

Two days after the incident, the *Las Vegas Optic* covered it in more detail and revealed that Sario Gonzales and his business had received unwanted attention as a result.

Miguel Sedillo was cut and seriously wounded in a brawl Sunday afternoon at the Swastika Saloon near the sawmill late Sunday night, attempted to dress and make his escape from the jailer's room at the county jail, where he was being kept because it was feared to move him. Sedillo almost died while his wounds were being sewn up Sunday afternoon, and that he was even able to leave his couch that night is a tribute to his marvelous vitality.

Sedillo was discovered before he had dressed himself. He had feigned a faint and, while supposedly lying unconscious, was, in reality, sitting up and trying to clothe himself. He was being kept in the jail's room because that was where he had been treated and because he could be kept more quiet there and have a better chance for recovery. It was expected that he would be removed to the hospital yesterday, but after his attempt to escape, the officers decided not to trust him there.

A warrant was sworn out yesterday afternoon and served upon Sario Gonzales, sometimes known as "Si" Gonzales, the proprietor of the Swastika Saloon. He is charged with selling liquor on Sunday. It has been demonstrated to the satisfaction of the sheriff's office that Gonzales' place was open shortly before the fight and that all four of the participants, Miguel Sedillo, his brother Celso, Juan Calderon, and Sidiaco Guerrero, were drinking in the resort. Their fight started inside the place, according to the testimony of several witnesses who have talked to the officers, and was continued outside. The actual cause of the brawl is unknown. All were partially drunk and probably do not know why they were fighting.

The three men who sustained cuts in the affray will all recover, though their gashes will disfigure them for life. Sidiaco Guerrero, who was only kicked and beaten, is already able to be about.

Justice of the Peace Jose E. Romero charged Sario Gonzalez with selling liquor on Sunday, based on the testimony of Celso and Miguel Sedillo, Juan Calderon and Sidiaco Guerrero, who were in a drunken brawl allegedly caused by the liquor they purchased from Gonzalez. Although Sario paid a fine for his crime, it wasn't until five years later that his business was put back in the spotlight after another stabbing occurred at the Swastika Saloon on April 29, 1917. The *Albuquerque Morning Journal* printed on April 29, 1917,

Miguel Sedillo, charged with stabbing Mariano Baca, was arrested yesterday morning at his home in Old Albuquerque by Deputy Sheriff Perfecto Armijo and Constable Albert R. Garcia.

Baca was stabbed shortly after 7 o'clock Friday night at the Swastika saloon, Twelfth Street and Indian School Road. Sedillo, according to witnesses, driving a knife blade into the left lung. Baca was reported yesterday to be resting comfortably, but he was not declared to be out of danger. Pneumonia may develop.

Sedillo was placed in the county jail. He will not be arraigned until county officers learn positively whether Baca will recover or not.

Sedillo, according to county officers, is a knife fighter and served a term in the penitentiary for stabbing a man named Maldonado to death nearly twenty years ago. Sedillo had a narrow escape from death a little less than two years ago When Ramon Ortiz, then constable of Old Albuquerque, shot him in the abdomen. Sedillo had drawn a knife and refused to drop it at his command, Ortiz said. Ortiz knew him to be a knife fighter and fired.

Tells of Stabbing.

Baca, Sedillo and another man were drinking at the Swastika early Friday night. Baca and Sedillo were discussing something—what the third man did not know. Under Sheriff R. L. Wootton learned yesterday. Baca and Sedillo drew away from the third man, the undersheriff was told, and the knife play took place shortly afterward with lightning-like suddenness. The third man said the discussion contained no warning that violence might be looked for.

Between 1880 and 1914, sex work was a legitimate business in Albuquerque. The city even provided licenses for it. It is said that the establishment

An early image of the Swastika Saloon and its location near the lumber yard. *Image courtesy of the Painted Lady Bed and Brew.*

continued to operate as an illegal brothel beyond this period until around the middle of the twentieth century. Apparently, there was a sign outside the saloon that could be flipped to alert those who were in the know when it changed from a drinking house to a bordello at night. But by 1918, city authorities had started to take notice. The *Albuquerque Morning Journal* printed on August 14, 1918,

> *Following the examination of three witnesses by the board of county commissioners yesterday afternoon in the hearing of complaints against S. Gonzales, proprietor of the Swastika Saloon, which charged him with permitting women to loiter about his saloon, the commissioners took the case under advisement.*
>
> *A second complaint against Peter Rodda, proprietor of a place familiarly known as Silva's in Tijeras Canyon, was continued until 2 o'clock Thursday afternoon owing to a clerical error in the filing of the complaint.*
>
> *The complaint against the Swastika at Twelfth Street and the Indian School Road was signed by Reuben Perry, superintendent of the school. The complaint alleged that women were allowed to loiter about the place and that it was a place of bad repute.*
>
> *Francis Wood appeared as attorney for the complainant, while W.C. Heacock acted as attorney for Gonzales. Heacock opened the proceeding with the statement that the complaint was incomplete and based merely on*

"information and belief." Wood answered the statement with the declaration that the complainants would attempt to prove that under his present license, Gonzales permitted the women to loiter at his place.

B.F. Armijo, an employee of the Indian school, was the first witness called. He asserted that the saloon is surrounded by a board fence, possibly eight or ten feet high. He declared that during the school's commencement period, he saw automobiles containing men and women drive into the stockade surrounding the saloon.

When questioned regarding the reputation of the saloon in the surrounding neighborhood, Armijo did not reply, as an objection to the question was raised by Commissioner Thomas R. Duran.

Albana Gutierrez, a woman who lives in the vicinity of the saloon, was the second witness. She declared she passed the place occasionally at night and that she often saw the automobiles containing men and women drive into the place. She declared that a week ago Sunday night, she saw one of these parties drive into the stockade and saw the men and women drinking on the outside of the building.

"Nearly every time I pass the place," she informed the commissioners through an interpreter, "I see them. I have seen men and women drinking in front of the saloon."

Mrs. Severa Fajarado, an aged woman, declared that "two Sundays ago" she saw men and women in cars drive into the stockade.

"Every Sunday, I see them," she said.

On motion of Col. Alfred Grunsfeld, chairman of the commission, the matter was taken under advisement.

The situation reached a tipping point two days later, and Sario Gonzales got off lightly. The *Albuquerque Morning Journal* reported on the outcome on August 16, 1918.

Attorney Wood said in regard to the Gonzales case that he had proven by a number of witnesses that women and men drove to the Swastika Saloon as late as 10 o'clock on Sunday nights and that he also had proved by reliable witnesses who live in the neighborhood of the saloon, that the arrival of the women at the saloon in automobiles with men, was a common occurrence. The commissioners maintained that this was not sufficient proof of the loitering of women but refused Wood permission to establish the reputation of the place through his witnesses. The saloon's license was not revoked.

Eventually, Sario became involved in the moonshine trade, smuggling it to Juarez, Mexico. Like many others during that era, the family stored their money on their property rather than trust the banks with it. Rumor has it there is still $28,000 unaccounted for and could be hidden beneath floorboards, in walls or around the grounds. A treasure hunt was held on the premises in 2014, but it yielded no results besides an empty coffee can that was found underneath the floorboards. Sadly, Sario died in 1927, before Prohibition ended.

The building then passed to Sario's only son, Charles Gonzales. The former saloon space on the west end of the property likely opened in the early 1930s as Charlie's Grocery. It morphed into a grocery store, which also still had the attached (still operational brothel), according to old timers in the Wells Park neighborhood. Residents recall walking past the "bordello" as children to buy candy from the store. This would indicate that despite the ban in 1914, sex work still occurred there. The owner, Charlie, passed away in 1982, but his son, Charles "Bromo" Gonzales, opened a grocery store in the Barelas neighborhood called Bromo's Grocery. One of Bromo's sons, Michael Gonzales, went on to open the well-known Barelas Coffee House in 1978 at 1502 Fourth Street Southwest in the Barelas Neighborhood, an area it still occupies today.

Soon after Charlie's Grocery shut down, Charlie's granddaughter Benita Villanueva, with her husband, Vincent, transformed the building again when she renovated it into a private home and office. At some point after that, the building was renovated again, this time converted into a triplex with three apartments. To finish the transformation, a drop ceiling eight feet in height. covered the original lofty ceilings, and the hardwood floors were overlaid with shag carpeting and linoleum tile. A chain link fence was placed around the long adobe structure, and it started to be forgotten little by little until 2014, when Jesse Herron bought it. He graciously shared stories about the building's shadowy history and discovered that the building was haunted.

When I bought it in 2014, a previous owner did a renovation, possibly in the latter half of the twentieth century. They added a drop ceiling, carpet and linoleum tile, cloaking pretty much any historical significance. But luckily, when we pulled up the carpeting, it had protected the one-hundred-plus-year-old wood floors, some with bloodstains and strange markings on them. So, we lucked out! We peeled it back to its original layout of being a saloon and brothel as best we could. We added bathrooms because, back then, they didn't have indoor plumbing. There were privies out here in the yard.

I had an appraiser come here while doing a construction loan in 2014. She had to measure the entire property. She said, "You're not going to believe this, but the saloon part is exactly 666 square feet."

Originally, there was a back door and a long hallway that ran the entire length of the property, which is probably 130 feet long. It's a single-story structure with 11-foot-tall ceilings. So, it's about 3,000 feet square feet total. A long hallway bisected the entire property, leading from the "wine room" saloon to the brothel rooms. Guests would enter the saloon via the front door. The hallway was located just behind the bar. Basically, it was an eight-room brothel, with four rooms and what might have been parlors or waiting rooms on each side. The hallway does not exist anymore, but you can still see the original door frames that led to it. The brothel rooms had dirt floors when I moved in. It was a "crib" brothel, which was pretty much the worst of the worst. I think the wood floors were just in the waiting areas. I believe that the women who worked here lived here as well.

The saloon was right across from the American Lumber Company sawmill. It was a time in Albuquerque's history when there were probably ten men to every lady. With the blue-collar workforce across the street, I'd imagine this place was always busy.

Jesse also says that the building is "pretty darn haunted."

I lived here for nine years in the owner's suite, now named Jessie [named after him but with the female spelling]. *It was entertaining the first year or so, feeling like "what's going to happen tonight." That entertainment factor wore off fairly soon. It got pretty bad. It was really, really bad the final year* [2022], *where things were happening every night. I developed a real anxiety about going to sleep here. I've only been scared here a few times, but it was mostly annoying because they would enter the room. I wouldn't be going to sleep till two or three in the morning because I had this anxiety about falling asleep. And sure enough, the ghosts would come in, and I'd hear them. They're clumsy. They're moving things, they bump into stuff, they make noise. They would come up on the bed and you could feel the mattress move slightly. If it wasn't moving, it would be vibrating.*

For a long time, even from the first nights of my living here, something would come into the room, and it would lay on the bed next to me. Ghost Adventures [a television show] *came here in 2020 and filmed during the pandemic. I invited my neighbor, Samantha Madrid, to take part in the filming. Her family built this place in the 1800s. She has a strong connection to it. She grew up next door. She now lives there with her kids as an adult. So, she came over for the filming of* Ghost Adventures *for*

The Painted Lady Bed and Brew as it appears today. *Photograph by the author.*

A photograph taken during the cleansing of the building. *Image courtesy of the Painted Lady Bed and Brew.*

the walkthrough with the interview and stuff. She owns a business called Sakrid Moon, where she earns her living as a psychic.

As I was talking to her, thanking her for her involvement in the taping, she told me that there's a "Lolita" that crawls into bed with me at night. I simply told her, yes, I know. It's happened since the first night I ever slept there. I would often feel her come into the room and lie down on the bed. And it's not like a human's weight. It is the size of a human, but the mass feels like a cat coming on the bed. The mattress will move and depress, but not like the weight of a human. I'll feel her energy at other times because she has a particular energy, a comforting energy. Occasionally, she'd be on the bed next to me. On one occasion, I felt her floating above my head on the pillow. I saw her once, and she is the one apparition I've ever seen here. She revealed herself to me because she was protecting me from something negative and harmful in the room. She looked between the ages of twelve and eighteen. I was arm's length from her. She was right at my bedside table. I made sure I was awake because I've been here for so long that I do a check when something ghostly happens. I checked the time on my clock and looked right at her. She wouldn't look at me. She didn't make eye contact. She just looked very stoically straight forward. I could see her eye makeup. Her hair was pulled back in a tight bun, and she was Hispanic. She was young looking, and I thought she had a mother who worked here, or maybe she worked in the saloon and would bring beer or whiskey to the men.

Living here, I've met a handful of psychics and mediums, and they've been through here. One came a couple years ago, and she said a little girl is here. And I asked if she could see her. She described her exactly as I saw her. And she said they made her look older than she actually is. She was a prostitute here.

Jesse's girlfriend, Candy, also spoke of some paranormal occurrences in the building.

Jesse and I had been out doing a little brewery crawl, but we were sober. We didn't have too much to drink, and we were up late. We didn't get home till midnight. We were up late chatting, and it was probably 1:30-ish in the morning. We're just sitting there chatting, and he is telling me the stories about the painted lady, the things he's experienced living here and the shows filmed here, things that have happened. Then he asked me if I had any ghostly experiences. I said, "No negative ones. Perhaps some people that have passed that I felt have returned and given me a sign or something." So, we're in mid-conversation, and we heard this massive crash in the living room. It was loud, and we could just hear something falling and breaking, so we ran out to the living room.

A few years ago, a show called That's Some Scary Sh!t *was filmed here, and he had a movie poster from when they filmed it. It flew completely off the wall mid–ghost story. As he's telling me a ghost story, it's on the wall and came soaring off. There's glass that's shattered everywhere—I mean glass covering the entire front room. And strangely enough, it was Friday the thirteenth.*

We walked over there, and Jesse was trying to figure out what had happened. He thought maybe it's humidity, maybe it's this. Maybe it might have fallen, but this, like, flew off. It's way over here. Like, there's probably no way. That was my first major experience of something very odd happening.

The next one was probably the scariest for me. Jesse was cleaning rooms, so I watched TV in the apartment. In the apartment, at that time, Jesse had these little plates hanging over the sink, these little portion plates. On his stove, there were spices and other things. I'm just sitting there watching TV, and everything flies off the wall. All the plates come crashing down. They're all on the floor of the kitchen.

The spices all fell, lying flat on the stove, and he's in the next room over cleaning. And so, I called him, telling him to get back into this room immediately. All your plates are on the floor. Some of them had broken. He also had this little plant hanging from the ceiling, and the planter was swinging back and forth. Whatever's happening in here, you must come talk to them. I can't do this by myself.

Next, we went into the Jesse Suite, the room that Jesse believes is the most haunted and where he continues his story.

So, we're in the bedroom right now where, at some point in the 1800s, this story was passed down through the family that owned it. A man came into this room from the outside and saw his lover, wife or girlfriend. I don't remember the story precisely with the other man. So, he went back home, grabbed an axe, came back in here and just hacked them both to bits. And then he walked out the door right behind you and shot himself in the head and killed himself.

When I first moved in here, you would walk right through the threshold, and the energy was just so strong and just dark. And my dog didn't like coming into this room. He was scared.

I had this place cleansed for the first time in 2014. We had this Buddhist priestess come, and we were in this room here, and she said there are three spirits in here, two of them are female and one male. She said she was going to help them cross over.

So, after she does her thing, she says there's one more spirit here, a man, and he hides in the corner. She pointed to this corner, where there was a couch and a plant. She said he hides in the corner, and he's not going to go. The two women crossed over. I think they were former prostitutes. However, the energy felt incredibly different. It felt great. It was positive. My dog, Bill Murray, a three-legged greyhound mix was hopping around again, and it felt good. And so, I thought, "Well, two out of three ain't bad. We can all live together. We'll have a little arrangement because I don't blame him. This is his house, too."

You can stay in the room where the saloon was once located. *Photograph by the author.*

A few months later, a group of psychics showed up at my door, and I was walking them through. We are on the outside, and one of them is touching the original interior brothel doors that I have placed outside as a gate. She said, "You've had this place cleansed before." And I said yes. She then told me there were three ghosts but only two left. I was shocked but told her there was one other spirit in here, but we were cool. We have an understanding.

"You're not cool," she said. "He's angry that you're still here because all the other owners never lasted this long. The longer you let him stay here, the more power he builds. And when you're not around, he's tormenting your dog and aging your dog." That bothered me. That's where you draw the line. You can mess with me, but you're not messing with Murray, you know?

So, I asked her if there were ways to force it out. Because we tried. She gave me her phone number, and things were getting really bad a couple days later. So, she returned with her partner, and they set up a little demon trap in the living room.

So, they basically do a cleansing and light this trap on fire. Soon, she's got the spirit cornered, and she is trying to drive it into the flames of this trap. She was asking its name because she said if she knows its name, she has more power to expel it. However, the thing would not tell her its name, but she said all the other spirits in the house shouted "Bill!" So, apparently, he was a really negative spirit, oppressing all the other good spirits in the house. So, they were like outing him by calling out his name. She heard them all say "Bill, Bill, Bill!" And she said, as he was going into the trap, she could see him, and he was dressed like somebody from the late 1800s with a top hat, and he was clawing at her, trying to bring her with him into the demon trap.

As soon as he went, things felt really good. So, she put chlorite over all the transom windows, all the entrances, all the doors and black tourmaline in the corners to create a grid so nothing bad can come in and get in here.

A few months later, I noticed Murray, my dog, watching something. Animals

A demon trap was used to remove some of the nastier spirits. *Image courtesy of the Painted Lady Bed and Brew.*

are really intuitive, and he was looking at something right above the bed, where the ceiling meets the wall. He was clearly agitated. And I was like, "No, we're good. It's been cleansed. It feels great."

A couple nights later, I was sleeping and having this weird dream. I woke up and saw in my mind's eye this thing come down the hallway, and it crawled up one wall, down the other and then came down on me. It felt like it was trying to possess me. I was wide awake and was fighting it off mentally. I was fighting it off physically, and I was able to get it off.

I sat up in bed and turned the lights on, and this black-like figure was at the edge of the bed. Murray was awake and looking, and his ears were perked up.

So, I called them back, the ones that did the demon trap. I told them that something else had come in. She returned and said, "Yes, there's something else here." And she did the demon trap again, but it was a bigger trap this time. After a while she said, "OK, it's gone." And I said, "Did it go in the trap?" And she said, "No, it went out the window. It's not coming back here, but it's going somewhere else."

I asked if she could see it. She said she could and asked if I really wanted to know. I said, "Well, I think I saw it, so yeah." She told me that Bill was once human but this was never human. This was a demon. She said that it presented itself as a long, dark lizard. And it's precisely as I saw it, like this long six- to eight-foot thing that crawled on the wall. She said it was a succubus. I replied, "Well, we created this grid. It was supposed to keep out all these things." Then she said, "You invited it in." And I said, "No, I didn't." But she remained adamant and said, "No, you said, 'Come on in.'" I asked her how long ago, and she said it was a month ago.

I looked at my phone and had a friend come over who I hadn't seen in months. And he was having a really difficult time with work and life troubles. He was just negative. He came over to go on a bike ride, and he knocked on the door, and I said, "Come on in." I think it was attached to him. And he came in here and dropped it off. And then his life got really good. And then it got real, real dark for me and Bill Murray. You know, being attacked in your sleep is not fun.

The absolute most amazing thing happened while living there, too. This occurred on February 21, 2020. I was awoken by a loud bang and a whooshing sound coming out of my bed's headboard. (I made the headboard out of one of the old interior brothel doors about a year or two prior). As soon as my eyes adjusted to the darkness of the room, I could see these various-sized shapes, all one-dimensional, moving in a counterclockwise rotation around the room. It filled the room with hundreds, maybe thousands, of them from floor to ceiling. They were blacker than the black of the room—it was as if no light could escape them. I remember very consciously making sure that I was awake and taking note of everything that I saw. After about five minutes of me watching these shapes, I simply went back to sleep. I wasn't scared and it didn't feel threatening. I think it was a portal opening; all the shapes were spirits or entities coming through. It was like the universe was putting on a spectral display for me, one that no human ever gets to see. It was awesome!

Fortunately, the bad spirits were eventually driven from the property. However, it is believed that a few docile ones may remain. In 2015, the space underwent a significant renovation and was opened as Painted Lady Bed and Brew. It distinguishes itself from traditional bed-and-breakfasts,

Enjoy local Albuquerque craft beer daily from the storied grounds of a nineteenth-century former brothel and saloon. *Photograph by the author.*

offering beer instead of breakfast. On International Beer Day, August 3, 2018, Painted Lady Bed and Brew opened its doors. This establishment was lovingly created to bring people together over a beer. Beer has an "every man" image, one that's centered on community and unity, which makes it particularly inviting and accessible. It has the unique ability to create social connections and build feelings of togetherness. But don't be shocked if you come across spirits of a nonalcoholic variety.

BIBLIOGRAPHY

Baylor, Dorothy J. "Folklore from Socorro, New Mexico." *Hoosier Folklore* 6, no. 3 (1947): 91–100. http://www.jstor.org/stable/27649891.

Bryan, Howard. "Off the Beaten Path." *Albuquerque Tribune*, October 29, 1959.
————. "Off the Beaten Path." *Albuquerque Tribune*, October 31, 1978.

City of Dust. "The Shaffer Hotel, Mountainair, New Mexico." https://cityofdust.blogspot.com/2012/01/shaffer-hotel-mountainair-new-mexico.html.

Harden, Paul. "Haunted Socorro." *El Defensor Chieftain*, October 31, 2009.
————. "Haunted Socorro." Visit Socorro. https://www.socorronm.org/notable-local/haunted-socorro/.

Melzer, Richard. "The Belen Harvey House and Its Several Reincarnations,1910 to 2010." http://www.donaanacountyhistsoc.org/HistoricalReview/2011/ThreeHistoricalReview2011.pdf

Painted Lady Bed and Brew. "History." https://www.breakfastisoverrated.com/history

Polston, Cody. "Shaffer Hotel, Mountainair, NM (History)." https://www.codypolston.com/shaffer-hotel-mountainair-nm-history/.

Texas Escapes. "Civil War in the Southwest." https://www.texasescapes.com/JefferyRobenalt/Civil-War-in-the-Southwest.htm.

Thompson, Fritz. "Ghost, Ghosts, Ghosts." *Albuquerque Journal*, October 30, 1979.

"Von Ormy in the Civil War: The New Mexican Campaigns." *Von Ormy Star*, July 12, 2013. http://www.vonormystar.com/2013/07/von-ormy-in-civil-war-new-mexican.html

ABOUT THE AUTHOR

Cody Polston is an amateur historian who enjoys providing guided tours of Albuquerque and other ancient places in the American Southwest. He has been featured on numerous radio and television programs, such as *Dead Famous* (Biography Channel), *Weird Travels* (Travel Channel) and *In Her Mother's Footsteps* (Lifetime Channel exclusive), as well as *Extreme Paranormal* and *The Ghost Prophecies* (A&E Network). Cody has written numerous books regarding the history of the Southwest, ghost stories, paranormal fiction and fantasy.